SUCK A LITTLE HAPPY JUICE

AN IRREVERENT, BY-THE-SKIN-OF-YOUR-TEETH
GUIDE TO BEING AN INDIE AUTHOR

J. SCOTT COATSWORTH

Published by
Other Worlds Ink
PO Box 19341, Sacramento, CA 95819

❀ Created with Vellum

CONTENTS

About This Book   vii

PART ONE
IN THE BEGINNING

A Little Philosophy: You're Only as Thick as Your Skin   3
So You Wanna Write   5
Building a House   9
Hitting The Beats (It's a Marathon, Not a Sprint)   12
Breaking the Rules   15
There Are No New Ideas. Or Are There?   18
About Generative AI   21

PART TWO
YOU OUGHT TO KNOW

A Little Philosophy: Balance   27
I Wish I'd Known   29
The Eight Phases of Writing   34
Writing Short vs. Writing Long   37
Writing What You (Don't) Know   39
Plantsing   41
Writing in First Person   44
Writing in Third Person   47

PART THREE
DIVING IN

A Little Philosophy: Immerse Yourself In Your New World   53
Diving Into Your Characters   55
Damage   60
Building a World   63
Details Matter   65
Procrastination and Chocolate   67
Writer's Wait   69
The "Holy Shit" Moment   72
Facing Down a Deadline   74
Remembering to Shower   77
Rediscovering the Joy   79

PART FOUR

TRICKS AND TIPS

A Little Philosophy: The Power of Downtime	85
40 Tips For New Writers	87
Upping the Odds	93
The Wolf Under the Table	95
Keeping a Series Bible	98
A Full-Time Writer With Part-Time Time	103
Spice Up Your Story With Slang	106
Technobabble	108
When The Word Is the Story	110
Hiding Easter Eggs	113
Suck a Little Happy Juice!	115

PART FIVE

READY, EDIT, GO!

A Little Philosophy: Gardening is Writing	121
The Fixit List	123
Why I Love Second Drafts	127
Why You Need Some Good Beta Readers	130
Sense & Sensitivity	133
The Perfect Title	136
Should You Become an Indie Author?	139
If You Submit	145

PART SIX

GETTING IT OUT THERE

A Little Philosophy: Being On Brand	149
The Netflix Effect	152
Narrow or Wide?	154
Shaking Up Your Marketing Plan	158
Writing For a Blog Tour	162
Reading to the Crowd	165

PART SEVEN

GROUPS & EVENTS

A Little Philosophy: The Pink Flower	171
Making Connections	174
Preparing for the Con	176
Creating a Local Writing Community	181

Running a Group Sales Table - Part 1: Planning for the
Event   184
Running a Group Sales Table - Part 2: The Pregame and
the Event Itself   189

PART EIGHT

REVIEWS & REALITY CHECKS

A Little Philosophy: Small Joys   199
The Waiting Game   201
F@ck the Reviews   204
Imposter or Bust   208

What We Do Matters   211
Why I Wrote This Book   215
Author Interview Questions   217
Recommended Resources   225
Glossary   227
About the Author   233
All of Scott's Books   235

ABOUT THIS BOOK

So you probably saw this book on the shelf, or on a website somewhere while searching for some advice on how to be an indie author—someone who publishes their own work—and thought "Suck a little happy juice? What the $%#@!does that mean?"

Let me enlighten you.

I started my professional writing journey in 2013, and in May of 2015, I launched my own blog—a place where I could talk about life, the universe, and share with my readers the meaning of being a writer and an author.

A few years later, I transitioned from having a publisher to being a hybrid author, meaning I publish my own work *and* have some titles with by a traditional publisher.

In the last decade or so, I have written close to 450 columns on the blog, many of them about the ins and outs—emotional, spiritual and practical—of being my own publisher.

One of those columns in particular really struck a chord when I wrote it, and I *knew* it would eventually become the title of this book. It was called "Suck a Little Happy Juice," and it was an exploration of the need to hold on to all the good things that happen during your indie author journey—reviews, kind words, great sales—and using them as a fuel and a panacea to keep yourself going when things get rough. From that chapter in this book:

> We need to bottle up all those great things and put them away, ready to be opened at a later date when things don't seem quite so rosy. When imposter syndrome runs us down, it's time to grab that "bottle" of "all the great things," off the shelf.
>
> Got a rejection? Open that file and relive some of those wonderful things folks said about you and your writing.
>
> Latest book sales in the gutter? Take a ride on the happy memory train.
>
> Hit with a horrendous edit? Suck a little happy juice.
>
> With life and the world in such a weird, precarious, and sometimes downright awful place, you have to grab the good when you have it.

This book a celebration of the joys of being your own publisher boss, a balm for those difficult times when it doesn't seem quite so glorious, and a warm blanket for when you feel left out in the cold by the book business.

I hope that it makes your indie author journey just a little easier and more enjoyable.

I wanted to thank a few people who were instrumental in making the book happen—Allison Behrens, who helped me clean up a mess of a manuscript imported from blog posts; Jaime Lee Moyer, who provided the idea for the entire first section of this book, among other things; Kelley York at Sleepy Fox Studio, who translated my ramblings into a beautiful cover; and Anara Guard, who marked up the Advance Proof with all those little typos that always slip through the cracks. And of course my husband Mark, who is always there for me. Love you all.

PART ONE
IN THE BEGINNING

So you want to write. Or if you're like me, you _need_ to write. Need it like you need to breathe, to eat, to enjoy true beauty in this world. Writing is not for the faint of heart though, and before you start to plan your first story, there are a few things you ought to know.

Although this is not a comprehensive list—that could fill a book of its own! Instead, I'll share with you a few things you may not have learned on your own otherwise before starting out into the crazy world that is book publishing.

If you're already an established writer, you may want to skip ahead to section three. But who knows? You may find this whole introductory thing to be entertaining. Stranger things have happened.

A LITTLE PHILOSOPHY: YOU'RE ONLY AS THICK AS YOUR SKIN

"The truth is, publishing will break your heart, but you can't let that stop you. You need to be tough. Really tough, or take your scribbles and go home. Becoming a writer isn't a stroll through the park, with bluebirds singing and cute animals running by your side. It's the freaking Thunderdome. Bring armor."

—JAMIE LEE MOYER, AUTHOR AND EDITOR

Publishing is famously called the lowest paid profession for a reason. And writers, especially newbies, are at the bottom of the barrel. There are literally millions of us, many quite talented, and with the ease of indie publishing these days and the advent of generative AI, it's harder than ever to get your work in front of a wide array of readers.

Authors are also creative types, and like most artists, we're predisposed to believing the worst about ourselves. There's even a name for it —Imposter Syndrome. I'll talk more about it, but basically it means that at any given moment, you might suddenly be seized by painful waves of self-doubt, questioning why you ever thought you were good enough to be an author.

Something else that's typical of us writer types—one bad review can wipe away all the confidence-boosting effects of ten great ones.

If you're reading this book (thank you!), it means you're serious about being a writer, and if you're anything like me, it's because you have to write. You probably discovered reading at a young age and thought, "I want to do that. I *need* to do that."

I'm only happy when I'm writing. Okay, not always at the exact time that I am putting words down on the page. But if I'm not writing regularly, I feel off. And when I am, things are just better.

But it's a double-edged sword. We work so hard to become good at this thing we do, and make it so easy for others to tear us down.

So if you really want to make this your career (like you have any choice), you'll need to find a way to make peace with your doubts.

I'm going to try to convince you of something that's totally counterintuitive. Doubt is not the enemy. Doubt is your friend. It spurs you on to constantly try to improve your writing skills, to become better at what you do.

To put it another way… once you stop doubting yourself, when you are convinced you know everything you need to know about being a great writer, your growth withers and dies.

In almost every project I write, I hit the patch I call the Muddy Middle, the place in the story where it all just feels derivative, sad, and boring. I've learned over the years that this is just part of my process. Once I plow through it, things get better, and I remember that I do actually have some idea what I'm doing.

And then the appearance of my nemesis becomes something more akin to the visit of an old friend.

So be ready for adversity. Prepare yourself for crushing waves of self-doubt. Expect reviews that will make you cry.

You'll find a way through it. Make a few close writer friends and talk to them about your travails. Remind yourself that writing is as much a part of you as your heart and soul, and that nothing will sway you from your chosen path.

And get the best revenge. Write some more.

Are you ready to do this? Let's dive in.

SO YOU WANNA WRITE

Maybe you were a writing whiz in high school, and finished your first novel before you were eighteen. Or maybe, later in life, you discovered your great desire to pen fascinating stories that everyone will want to read.

No matter when and where you start, you'll need to learn the basics before your writing can soar.

There Are (Weird, Contradictory) Rules

The history of writing goes back almost as far as humankind, with ancient civilizations employing cuneiform and hieroglyphs to tell stories and communicate information verbally. And since you're not (I'm guessing) Mesopotamian, you probably share your own ideas in English and/or other modern spoken and written languages.

These languages have rules. English, especially, has a mess of them, and I do mean a *mess*. Our tongue is a hodgepodge of different languages, something that results in some truly weird things.

Ever heard this one?

"What does GHOTI spell?"

It spells "fish." And before you tell me that's impossible, consider.

If you use the *"gh"* from *enouGH*, the *"o"* from *wOmen*, and the *"ti"* from *acTIon*, together they form something that sounds very convincingly like "fish."

Another example... did you know English has a very specific (and complicated) *order-of-adjectives* rule that applies whenever we use more than one adjective to describe a single noun? I didn't realize this until an Italian friend asked me why I was putting one adjective in particular before another. I looked into it, and lo and behold, I discovered this:

In English, adjectives must be placed in a very specific order by *opinion, size, age, shape, color, origin, material,* and *purpose*. That's eight levels to remember—no wonder ESL learners have such a hard time with the language.

Don't believe me? How does "the red big house" sound to your ears? How about "the metal old car"? Like nails on a chalkboard, I'm betting.

I must have learned this in grammar school at some point, because I do it instinctively, though things do get a bit hairy when I get into the four-five adjective territory. But who ever uses that many at once?

My point here is that you need to have a strong grasp of your native grammar before you write (and then submit) your first story. An obvious lack of grammatical skills will get your story thrown right into the rejection bin.

The Letters Go in a Certain Order

You also need to make sure you *spel your wirds* correctly.

See what I did there? It's jarring when a word is so clearly spelled wrong.

Few editors will bounce your story for an error or two, but turning in a manuscript with multiple misspellings signals that you are not serious about your craft. And if you don't take it seriously, why should they do the same for you?

We're not all good spellers, but there are many tools to help you catch these kinds of errors, as well as various grammatical ones. All the major word processors flag potential issues, and there are a number of add-on grammar apps that can help too.

I also find it helpful to read the story out loud (or use an app to read it to you) before I submit it. This engages a different part of your brain than typing does, and can help you ferret out misspellings and other errors you might otherwise miss.

Genres: A Conversation Between Readers and Writers

You'll also need to train yourself to write fiction in your chosen genre. Each one has its own conventions and expectations.

Most of the chapters in this book started out as blog posts, with a much different tone—very casual and self-referential ("in my book x I did y") because my initial audience was mostly my own adoring fans. Thanks to both of you!

In translating them from *blog* to *non-fiction book* style, I had to consider a different audience—writers of all stripes who probably don't know me from a hole in the ground. And so I adjusted the writing accordingly, removing many of the references to my own works, and adopting a more professional, though still hopefully welcoming, tone.

Similarly, each fiction genre has its own style, expectations, and inside jokes—a shared vocabulary built up over decades (and sometimes centuries) of writers and readers sharing ideas. These shift over time as the genres evolve. If you haven't already, read as many books as you can in your target genre both older works and brand-new ones, and get in on that conversation.

Make it Look Pretty—and Professional

Finally, when you're ready to submit, you'll need to know the current formatting norms. When I first started writing, about *mumble mumble* years ago, all submissions were done on paper, sent through the mail. Two spaces were expected between each sentence, italics had to be formatted as underlines, and the story needed to be printed in Times New Roman or Courier, fonts that mimicked the old typewriters.

Nowadays, submissions are done almost exclusively electronically, one space between sentences is standard, and only the most diehard of old-school editors still require underlines instead of italics.

Most editors and submission pages will refer you to William Shunn's manuscript formatting pages—the de-facto gold standard for story formatting. Shunn is a Hugo Award winning author of short fiction who has compiled a comprehensive set of fiction formatting guidelines. You'll find this and more helpful resources at the back of this book.

Take a Deep Breath

Does this all sound like a lot? It is, but it's something you can work on bit by bit as you go. Being a writer is a marathon, not a sprint. You're reading this because you have a burning desire to be a published author. The first step toward reaching that goal is to write *something*—to get all those thoughts swirling around in your head down onto the paper in story form—and then put it out there.

Just be ready for the Universe (in the form of beta readers, editors, and your best friend Chloe) to chime in and tell you where you still need work.

Writing is learning, and when you stop learning, your writing stagnates. So open yourself up to the Universe and start writing.

And congratulations! You're one of us writer folks now, and your life will never be the same.

BUILDING A HOUSE

n writing, there are many different forms, or structures, to choose from when you decide to write something new. Which one you use depends on the story you want to tell.

It's like building a house.

Maybe you have one person's story to tell, something that takes place over a fairly short period of time. You might choose to build a small studio apartment, where everything has its place and nothing that isn't necessary is included. That's a short story, usually anything up to 15,000 words.

Maybe you want to tell the story of a couple characters, but still over a very short time frame. You want a little more elbow room, but you'll still have to keep things reasonable. So you choose a two-bedroom apartment, where you can add a bit more in terms of furnishings and embellishments, but you'll still need to remain cognizant of your overall size. That's a novelette or novella, usually 15,000-40,000 words.

Or maybe you have something more ambitious in mind—the story of a grand event, or a tale told over a longer period of time in which our inhabitants must learn, interact, and grow. You might select a four-bedroom house on a decent plot of land, with views of the mountains in the distance. That's a novel, roughly 40,000-100,000 words.

Finally, maybe you are telling an epic story for the ages, one that sprawls out across time and/or worlds. One that requires a larger cast, each of whom has their own individual wants, motivations, and needs. If so, you might need a whole apartment complex, full of elevators and stairs and common areas where the characters might interact. That's an epic novel, which is usually more (and sometimes much more) than 100,000 words.

Each of these story structures has its own quirks and requirements. Short stories, for example, should make use of every single word, and this becomes truer the shorter the story. Writing flash fiction, for instance (usually 1,000 words or less), often entails a painstaking re-examination of the story to weed out unnecessary verbiage, extra sentences, or even changing out simple words for more complex ones that pack more into the story.

In the traditional short story format, it may be necessary to trim some of your gorgeous world building, and to limit the number of point of view characters. My general rule of thumb is one POV for a 5-10,000 word story, and two for 10,000-20,000.

Novellas offer you a bit more room to spread your wings, and can be much faster to write than a full-fledged novel. But beware... they often offer just enough story to get a reader hooked, while leaving them wanting more (and sometimes feeling cheated). I've received my share of "Loved this story but hated that it ended so soon" three-star reviews for my novellas.

Novels are my jam. They provide maximum room for exploration and even a bit of wandering—sure, head down that path through the enchanted forest and see where it leads—but your story's pacing matters even more here than in a shorter work. Just because you can meander a bit doesn't mean you should—you need to keep the trains running on time.

And epic-length novels? Don't get me wrong. As a reader, I love these. They let me really sink my teeth into a world for an extended period of time, which can be wonderful if you love the vibe the writer has created. But they're especially prone to wandering and faulty pacing. More isn't always more, and if you are writing at this length, you'll want to have a clearly established plot with enough regular movement to keep your readers engaged. You want them to think, "That's it?" when they finish, not "Thank God it's over."

So before you start in on your story, give it some thought, and decide if it's more suited to a chic studio apartment in town, a large ranch house out in the suburbs, or maybe even a castle with a moat on a faraway hill.

And if you choose the wrong one? Don't worry. You can always relocate.

HITTING THE BEATS (IT'S A MARATHON, NOT A SPRINT)

One of the hardest tricks to learn when writing novels is pacing. It's a little easier with a short story—at 5,000-15,000 words, it's harder for readers to become bored with your characters' exploits. But with a novella or novel, pacing becomes more important.

The classic example of a pacing template comes from the Romance market. Once upon a time, there were very specific plot expectations* laid out for Romance books by the major Romance publishers:

- The characters meet
- They're in denial about their connection
- They decide to give it a chance
- They date
- There's a big crisis and a break-up
- Something forces them back together
- They fall *hard* for each other
- They break up
- One or both of them make a sacrifice
- There's a declaration of love
- The Happily Ever After

Each of these is a *beat*—a step or shift in the plot. In classic Romance, publishers required that each these had to occur at a specific point or chapter in the story. It was a bit too structured for my taste, but taken together, these beats provided a road map for writing a satisfying romance.

These days, things are a bit looser, but the basic thinking still applies. Your plot consists of a series of individual events that all link together to craft a larger narrative, your overall story.

Let's take the original Star Wars film as an example:

Luke's boring Tatooine life is interrupted by a pair of lost droids carrying an important secret (beat 1). While out to search for one of them, he encounters the mysterious Ben Kenobi (beat 2). When he returns home, he finds his adoptive parents dead (beat 3) and that sends him fleeing to Mos Eisley where he meets a handsome rogue, Han Solo (beat 4). Luke and Ben convince Han to take them to Alderaan, and fall into a trap, as the Millennium Falcon is scooped up by the Death Star's tractor beam (beat 5).

I could go on, but you can see the point. Each of these events/beats is a carefully orchestrated plot point that leads the reader through the story.

Your story's beats and scenes don't all have to be action-based or fast-paced. It's just as important to give the reader a little break between your action sequences as it is to hurl them through space at warp speed.

We see an example of this in Luke's tinkering with R2D2 and managing the farm, which sets up the "normal" life Luke and his family live together. This makes it all the more poignant when that family is brutally massacred.

We get another break in the action when Luke is on the Falcon, learning the basics of how to use the Force.

Even though these scenes should be boring, they're not, because they convey key information about the plot to the reader—Princess Leia's secret message and the existence and uses of the Force.

When you're writing your own novel, you don't need to know exactly what these beats will be in advance, although some authors find it helpful to figure them all out before ever putting a pen to paper (or fingers to the keys).

Personally, I like to have a general idea of them when I start, and can shuffle them around as I go.

When the pacing seems a little slow, it usually means it's time to either impart some new information or to kick-start the action with a surprise beat and send your plot racing off in another direction.

As we've seen above, a good beat can come from several places: an unexpected event that shakes things up. A surprising revelation that provides new information or paints things in a different light. Or an encounter with someone new, who brings their own personality, baggage, and character interactions to the story. Look how Han's happy-go-lucky character changed the whole feel of the story.

If you know your characters well enough—who they are, where they came from, and what drives them, both past trauma and future goals—you can also mine this for plot beats too. What will happen when Luke, Han and Leia finally meet? Where will Luke's search for answers about his past take him? What logical plot beats will Han's rogue nature bring about, when the consequences of his lifestyle and constant rule-breaking finally catch up with him?

For my own stories, I keep a running chapter by chapter description of the plot so I can see more easily where things might be too slow (or too crazy-fast) and rectify them. This can be really hard to see when you're in the trenches, writing a chapter every few days.

As you're slogging through the long process of writing your novel, keep in mind what landmarks might lie ahead, and how you might use them to keep the story moving and your readers happy.

If you do it right, your plot will hum along steadily like a well-tuned spaceship.

Thanks to Robin Lovett's blog for the great list of romance plot beats.

BREAKING THE RULES

So many rules.

Every part of our lives is governed by them, and sadly writing is no exception.

There are rules of *grammar*:

- Always use the Oxford comma (the one after the second to the last item in a list).
- Never use the Oxford Comma (did I mention these rules are sometimes contradictory?)
- Always put closing quotes after the period, not before
- I before E, except after C, *except* when there's an exception to the rule

If you made it through high school English *and* you want to be a writer, you probably have a pretty decent handle on these rules. But there are others, too.

For instance, *formatting* rules, which can shift and change over time:

- Always underline your emphasized words and never use italics. Except that one has gone by the wayside now, and most places want you to italicize them instead
- Always put two spaces between sentences. This one's also gone. Now a single space is standard
- Always use Courier or Times New Roman, as those are considered eminently legible fonts. That one's still pretty standard
- Always indent the first line of your paragraph, but never, ever use tabs to do this. Tabs are the bane of editors everywhere. Instead, use Word's paragraph formatting options to create a first line indent of .5 inches
- Always separate scenes with a single, centered pound sign (#)

There are many more... for standard formatting guidelines, check out William Shunn's formatting guides online as I mentioned earlier—these have become industry standard.

There are rules for characters:

- The bad guy should have *some* redeeming qualities, or at least truly believe what they are doing is right
- "Good" characters need some flaws, or they end up being flat and boring
- Character details should be provided as much through their action and interactions as through their physical descriptions
- Refrain from "head-hopping"—jumping back and forth between characters' thoughts in a single scene

There are many more of these that the typical writer picks up in bits and pieces—rules for delivering information in a story, guidelines for creating good plots, helpful suggestions for story submissions, even proper etiquette for dealing with editors and beta readers.

But one thing to remember—these are rules, not laws. They are guidelines that thousands (even hundreds of thousands) of writers have come up with, many of them before you and I were even born. They shift and evolve over time, as they no longer prove useful or in vogue.

Pablo Picasso is purported to have said:

"Learn the rules like a pro, so you can break them like an artist."

Or in more simple language:

"Know the rule before you break it."

For every rule, there's someone who first mastered it and then found a *masterful* way to subvert it and turn it on its head. In an artist's hand, even poisonous lead can enliven a bright paint color that makes beautiful art. And even dirt can become a stunning sculpture.

So take your time to learn the ropes. Read some books on writing. Take some classes. Listen to your beta readers and editors and pick up the rules.

Then when you do decide to break them, you'll know exactly *why*.

THERE ARE NO NEW IDEAS.
OR ARE THERE?

sometimes pine for the early days of sci-fi, when everything was new. Each story idea shone with fresh brilliance, and many of the tropes we still use today were just being invented.

Sure, it was a much less diverse time. Yes, you had to write everything on a typewriter (they didn't even have correction fluid until the late fifties), and there was no such thing as self-publishing, or home computers, or Amazon, or the web in general.

Still, as a sci-fi writer in the mid-twentieth-century, you could sit down at your old Remington Portable typewriter (comes with its own leather case!) and chances were your idea had never before been set to paper. Think Asimov's three laws of robotics, Tolkien's Middle Earth, or Bradbury's iconic *Fahrenheit 451*.

In the intervening decades, we've advanced by leaps and bounds, technology-wise. Much of our tech is not so different from what many of these writers envisioned all those decades past (where are my flying cars and jetpacks, dammit?). Our cell phones are way better in many respects than the Star Trek's tricorders, though they still can't scan your body for injuries. And we've been to the moon and back, multiple times.

My point is that we live in a much different world today. So many amazing ideas have already been written down, made into TV series and movies, and pervaded the general consciousness. In this crowded field, it's hard to come up with something truly original.

This is not only true for science fiction. All of fiction benefits from an amazing abundance of writers and ideas, which often makes it hard to stand out in the crowded field. In addition, most traditional publishers really aren't looking for something *truly* revolutionary. They want the *last bestselling thing*, repackaged with a slightly different twist, that they can turn around and sell to the same people.

So what's an aspiring writer to do?

First, write what you are passionate about. Your enthusiasm for the genre and the story is one of the things that will set you apart from authors chasing the trends—almost always a losing battle. Believe in your story and commit to it wholeheartedly.

Second, read widely in your chosen genre(s), and figure out what folks are reading and liking these days. It's not so you can replicate the trends you find. It's to help you buck those trends and write something truly *different*, while being aware of what editors and agents have been looking for in the recent past.

Sure, you can just write a better version of what's already out there, and if that's your path to success, I commend you. But for me, I need a little magic, a bit of something different to really fire me up to write a story.

There are several ways to go about this.

Try mixing genres in an unexpected way. Zombies plus Jane Austen? Been done. But what about werewolves in the time of Julius Caesar? Or Witch-powered spacecraft? Or the invention of computers at the Library of Alexander? Some of today's most successful authors do so by mixing things up in an unexpected and exciting new way.

You can also flip a trope—take an expected plot point and turn it on its head. The Chosen One finds out they are the chooser. Or maybe the Sword of Destiny turns out to be something entirely different.

Ever read the *Sword of Shannara* (spoiler alert)? In Terry Brooks' original book, the sword turned out not to be a weapon of power, so much as an exposer of the truth of a death long denied. He took the trope of the magical sword and turned it inside out, making truth its ultimate weapon.

Once you've come up with a concept, write down a simple and clear explanation of what your story is about, something that encapsulates the cool new angle you've come up with that will set it apart. The best ideas can be explained succinctly, and that explanation can help guide you while writing your story.

In one of my own books, it was, "Humans return to the Earth from the moon, after a planet-wide apocalypse." In the fantastic film "The Map of Tiny Perfect Things," it's even simpler: "A teenaged boy stuck in a time loop discovers he's not the only one."

Idea creation these days is less a matter of bold new invention than the more subtle—but still satisfying—act of finding a niche that excites you. Try to blend some different combination of fiction ingredients and the world might just love it. If you can pull it off. In the end, it always comes back to the quality of the writing.

In 2013, a new band called Bastille put themselves on the musical map with a new song about… Pompeii. How? It was unexpected—a blend of Roman history and catchy pop music—and they had the skill to just make it *work*.

So go forth and read, take notes, and think about how you would tell the story *you'd* want to read.

Then sit down and write it.

ABOUT GENERATIVE AI

No book on indie writing in this day and age would be complete without a discussion of one of the most controversial topics authors and artists face today: generative Artificial Intelligence.

As a sci-fi writer, I have to explain that "generative AI" is not real artificial intelligence—at least not yet. There's little chance that it will go all Skynet on us and take over the world, at least not in the way that writers like me have imagined for decades. Instead, it's an advanced version of that function on your phone that guesses the next word you plan to type.

Generative AI, also known as Large Language Models, are essentially algorithms that work via pattern recognition. They are trained on millions and millions of samples, and they learn how these samples (whether they be language or images) are put together and then create new combinations at request.

In a perfect world, these samples would have been obtained legally, ethically, and with clear consent from their owners. Unfortunately, in our world, much of the material these apps have been trained on were vacuumed up off the web with little or no consent (often by changing site policies to allow the harvesting of users' photos and written work).

In at least one well-documented case, a company used a large pirated collection of books to train their own AI, including six novels by yours truly.

Because of these issues, every time you use generative AI in its current form, the work it generates is created on the backs of thousands of authors or artists without their direct consent, and in most cases without any compensation. And the US Copyright Office has indicated that it will not copyright any AI-generated works, leaving authors and artists who use them with little legal protection.

There are a few encouraging signs as of this writing. One large stock photo site is experimenting with a compensation model for images created using their licensed images. Several governments around the world are also working on a regulatory framework, but advances in generative AI may quickly outrace such efforts.

I flirted with this new technology in its early days, playing with one of the image generators and testing out one of the chat-based text services. Don't get me wrong—this is a fascinating, transformative technology.

But the more you get into it, the more you see that the work it creates doesn't have a soul. Images made from this technology are often bright and candy-colored and compelling, but they are also repetitive and hollow… spend a bit of time looking for a cover image on one of the stock photo sites, and you'll see what I mean.

And the text they produce, while often serviceable if a bit flat and pedantic, may work well for non-fiction uses. But most sixth graders could produce better fiction.

This technology is also deeply problematic, both because of the way it is being created and for the fact that it is already putting creative folks out of work.

AI-generated visual art is clogging up some of the major stock art services, and many cover artists have seen a sharp decline in paid work. AI-generated books are taking many spaces at our book sales platforms that used to go to folks like you and I who slaved for months to create a wonderful and unique story. And now AI has come for audiobook narrator jobs too.

I'm hopeful that this technology may someday become very useful in our day-to-day lives, assisting us rather than being used to replace us.

So I'd recommend sticking to your own brain (and real human artists) for your stories and covers. They should reflect you as a beautiful, singular, talented indie author, not a million other creators blended into one.

PART TWO
YOU OUGHT TO KNOW

Writing, at its heart, is all about getting the words down on the page. We'll start out with a few things you'll want to think about as you embark on your writing career.

A LITTLE PHILOSOPHY: BALANCE

You can write whatever you want.

No, seriously. You're a *writer*. If you want to write an epic novel about the fine mesh of belly button lint, or wax eloquent in a poem about how sunlight glints off the dewdrops on a dandelion in the early morning, or even share your deepest, darkest fantasies in print, you can do it.

That doesn't mean it's going to sell.

I once had a great idea for a fresh take on the King Arthur myth for a "legends" fantasy anthology. I ran it by the editor, a good friend of mine, just to make sure I was on the right track. My last story for that publisher ended up being a serious misfire, and although the situation ended well, I didn't want to make the same mistake.

She didn't *love* the idea.

"King Arthur has been done. And done and done and done." She acknowledged that it was possible to still bring something fresh to the story, but it was clear that she was already biased against it.

Now, the fact that it has already been done isn't necessarily a deal breaker for me. I like playing with tropes and ideas, including stories that other people think have already been driven into the ground. But when Michelle Visage tells you your dress is for shit, you'd better listen to her or you're going home.

It's very possible that I could have crafted a beautiful, original, compelling story using the King Arthur myth as a backdrop. It might make readers laugh and cry and giggle with amazement. But none of that would matter if it was rejected by the editor. Going down that path, I'd be starting the game with one strike against me.

Yes, I'm a writer. I can write whatever I want. But if I want to sell it, I have to pay at least a little attention to what the public wants, and before that, to what the editor is looking for.

It's a balance, one that you probably need to learn to strike, sooner or later, if you're going to be a successful author.

In the end, I chose another legend for this story, something a little less well-trodden. And it became a fabulous story that still delights my readers to this day.

And because I listened, it had much more of a chance to actually reach them.

Write what you want. But keep in mind that you might need to tweak it, so it has a chance to sell.

I WISH I'D KNOWN

Every writer has a list of things they wish they'd known when they started. Writing is a craft, like any other, and each mistake teaches us something new. Here are a few things I would tell my younger self if I could, knowledge that would have made my writing journey a little easier.

Rejections Happen. Don't Let Them Stop You: If you give up being a writer just because you received a few rejections, you've already lost the game. You may be awful at writing, or you might be the best writer who ever lived. Either way, you will be rejected, sooner or later (and probably a lot). It may not have anything to do with the quality of your writing, and even if it does, you can work on your skills and become a better writer. Most likely, your story just didn't connect with that editor at that particular time. I got rejected by ten big publishers when I was twenty-seven, and I let it derail my writing career for almost two decades. Don't do what I did. Believe in yourself and forge ahead.

It Doesn't Need to Be Perfect the First Time: Another newbie writer error is trying to make sure the story is perfect in its first draft. The perfect really is the enemy of the good. If you spend more than a week tweaking one page of your book (unless it's the first one and you're angling to snag an agent or big publisher with it), you've probably fallen into this trap. Let it go and keep writing. You can fix any issues in later drafts.

The Muddy Middle is Real: Many writers get bogged down in the story somewhere around the middle (for me it's usually two-thirds of the way through—what I call the "muddy middle"). What once seemed fresh and daring now seems hokey, trite, and overdone, and you can't ever see yourself selling the cursed thing. But take heart—maybe it sucks, maybe it doesn't. But it's all *fixable*. Stick to your goal, move on, and finish the story. Leave it to your future self to determine if it's really bad as you think. You might be surprised once you have a chance to get a little distance and perspective.

Start Out In The Market You Want To Be In: When I began writing seriously in 2013, my first submission was to some anthologies in the Romance market. Romance wasn't my first love—that would be sci-fi/fantasy. But publishers I knew about in that market had openings for stories that I knew how to write, and so I took a chance. While I don't regret my decision—I've made some amazing friends and published a bunch of great stories through those channels—I ended up spending years moving from the Romance market to the sci-fi/fantasy market. Figure out where you want to be, and focus all your efforts there.

Learn The Rules: There are a lot of rules to writing—and a lot of strong publisher and editor preferences, backed up by the various style guides. Since I've come back to writing, I've learned that double spaces between sentences are out, that I should *never* use semicolons and rarely use adverbs. Writers no longer underline italics, and in many genres rarely use "he said" or "she said," though this is still in vogue in literary fiction. So learn the rules first. But here's the thing, once you know them, you *can* break them. You just need to know why you're doing it, and for what effect.

Write What's In Your Heart: There's always some new, hot trend in the market. Werewolves, Mars, vampires, RPG, zombies, etc. But very few people are able to chase the market successfully—by the time you get there with your story, it has already moved on to something new. In the long run, you'll be happier writing the thing that makes *you* happy, even if it doesn't make you tons of money. And when you write what you like, your enthusiasm shines through your work, making it that much more likely that you will find success with it.

Make Friends—Lots and Lots of Friends: Networking is the lifeblood of this market. And while having lots of friends doesn't guarantee your success, it does give you connections and options. Identify editors, successful authors, and others in your specific niche and get to know them. Offer to help them with their own needs, sharing their work, beta reading for them, etc. and they will most likely return the favor. Build bridges, not walls.

Don't Read Your Goodreads or Amazon Reviews: Or if you do, bring along a friend and a bottle of whiskey to buffer the pain. We writers are notoriously thin-skinned. We wear our art on our sleeves, and one nasty review can obliterate ten five-star ones. Be *very* careful checking your reader reviews, especially at first. The writers who quit their craft after reading a single horrible review are legion. Don't be one of them.

Don't Be Afraid To Sell Yourself: You're an author. It's probably because you feel a deep-seated need to write—you have stories in your soul that need to be told. Be proud of it. How many people say they want to be writers and actually follow through with it? How many people actually put out a first book, or a second, or a third? You are a rare breed. Don't be afraid to promote yourself and what you do. There's a whole audience out there waiting to find you.

Don't Be Afraid Of The Tech: This one's especially important if you are indie publishing. The ability to indie pub has become so much easier in the last few years, but it's still daunting. When I published my first indie author book a couple years back, I bit my nails down to the quick, worried sick I was doing it wrong. But here's the good news. Remember all the friends I made you make above? Well, I'm betting at least one of them knows how to do each and every one of the technological things you'll need to learn, and is willing to help. So dive in, and call those life-lines when you need them. You'll figure it all out—I have faith in you.

Don't Expect to Become an Overnight Bestseller: Does it happen? Sure! Sometimes an unknown author strikes gold on their first try with exactly the right idea, decent writing, and the right contacts, all at the same time. But most of us slog along for years before we have anything approaching an overnight success. So it's nose-to-the-grindstone time. Write as much as possible, learn to be the best writer you can, and see where it takes you. Effort is often destiny.

Always Doubt Yourself: Okay, so I know this sounds weird. But I mean it in a good way. Be humble and remember that you can always improve your craft. I had the fortune to *not* hit it big with my first novel. It's easy when you find great success to start believing in your own mythology and writing ability. But a healthy streak of self-doubt keeps you striving to be better.

Support Your Fellow Writers: If you have a blog, offer it up for announcements of your writer friends' works, especially those who have audiences that overlap with yours. Cheer your fellow authors on when they have triumphs and console them when they fall. Build the community you want to be a part of—in the long run, it will pay you back.

Be Kind: Over your career as a writer, you're going to meet a bunch of wonderful people. You'll also meet a motley assortment of fools, assholes, jerks, and folks who are just happening to have a crappy day when they cross your path. Be nice. It costs you nothing, and over time will become a part of your brand and will be reflected in the way people treat you back. And when you do run across someone who makes you feel small, don't return the favor. Be kind to them. Have a couple of close friends you can vent to privately to blow off steam. And if someone persists in being a jerk, don't be afraid to block them from your social media. After all, "be kind" doesn't mean "be a pushover." It's just means putting out into the world what you want to see more of—a little light.

Celebrate the Wins: You'll have enough heartache and disappointment in your life as an author. So when you sell a book, or have one come out, or get a great review, stop and savor the moment. Get yourself a chocolate bar or glass of champagne. Go out to dinner with your honey. Take a long bubble bath and don't skimp on the bubbles. Do whatever makes you happy—you deserve it.

There are others I could share—particulars about how to manage backlist, where to distribute your books, etc. But starting with the basics will help you with your long-term plan, whatever challenges you end up facing.

Define your own success.

THE EIGHT PHASES OF WRITING

Almost every author goes through phases when writing a new work, especially a longer one. Although the details may vary a bit from author to author, the broad strokes are probably very similar.

Here are mine:

Phase One—The New Journey: This is the honeymoon phase. The story is fresh, and you just know you're going to knock it out of the park. Surely you can get this thing done in a few weeks—a month at most. And you don't need no stinking second draft.

Phase Two—The Slog: This is when you really start to get into the meat of the story. You realize that your characters can be really boring sometimes, and this may take more than a couple weeks. So you try to spice things up a bit—a surprise attack here, some breathtaking scenery there. But sooner or later, it hits you that you're just going to have to slog through the boring parts, and hope your readers will be willing to also.

Phase Three—The Great Idea: This is the part, usually about halfway though, when you are struck by *The Great Idea*—the twist that will give your story new life and redirect it to an ending that even a fortune teller with a time machine wouldn't be able to predict. Sometimes it's a paradigm shift. Sometimes one of your characters gets ornery and decides he'd rather be a barista. Or a space pilot. Or a tree. But you charge ahead, full of new energy.

Phase Four—My Writing Sucks: This is the worst phase of all. It's the point you reach, especially when you are on a deadline, when it suddenly dawns on you that you may not be able to finish it on time. That your whole story is basically just two guys walking through a forest. That *The Great Idea* you had in Phase Three didn't work out (it turns out trees can be quite boring as characters) and has totally screwed up half the things you said in the first part of the story. It's going to need editing. Like, a shit ton of editing. It's been two long months already, and the bloody thing still isn't finished. This is usually followed by Phase Four-B—crawl back into bed with a couple pints of ice cream.

Phase Five—I Totally Got This: This is when your natural writer's ego starts to reassert itself. "I'm almost there. I can do this." You get back to your desk and assess the damage, and (hopefully) it's not as bad as you feared. You dig back in and start to steer this unwieldy oil tanker of a novel into port. Then, just like that, you're done.

Phase Six—The Rewrite (AKA The Second Slog): This is the oh-my-gawd-don't-make-me-do-this part that most writers dread. You've already written the story. It's done. And now you have to read it *all over again*. Only slower. And you have to *make changes*. If you're like me, you rewrite almost everything, smoothing out the text, adding details, fleshing out scenes. And by the time you are halfway through, you start to wish you were dead. Or a firefighter. Or maybe a DMV worker. Anything but a writer. And if you are a perfectionist, there may even be a *third slog* in your future. Lucky you!

Phase Seven: The Submission: And finally, the-book-that-ate-your-life is out of your hands and off into the world. You breathe a huge sigh of relief. Once again, you have conquered the writing gods and channeled, if not a masterpiece, then at least a half-decent piece of fiction. You're done!

At least, until first edits come back.

And finally, one more phase:

Phase Eight—I *Can* Write!: This is the best one, the part where you go back and read your own stuff much later—maybe even months or years later. And it hits you that it's actually pretty damned good. It doesn't always happen—I've written a few stinkers. But when it does, it's almost as great as Phase One.

And all is right in the world again.

WRITING SHORT VS. WRITING LONG

For three years, I wrote two novels a year, and once that was done, I took a little break and set my sights on conquering SFWA (pronounced "SiffWah") aka The Science Fiction & Fantasy Writers Association.

At that time, there were a couple ways to become a SFWA member. I didn't have high enough sales for the first way, which required single book sales of a certain dollar amount in a twelve-month period for full membership. But there was a lower tier of membership that you could reach with short story sales in sci-fi markets.

So I wrote a bunch of shorts, and the process brought home to me the great difference between writing a short story and writing a full-length novel.

I world-build. I love creating a rich tapestry for my readers, done over the length of a novel in small pieces so that it's never overwhelming.

In a short story, you don't have the luxury to space things out. Nevertheless, I did my best to create fully realized worlds on a much smaller canvas in these shorts. It was a challenge, especially since some magazines I wanted to submit to had fairly low maximum word counts. I mean, seriously, five thousand words? I've written sentences longer than that.

So, as is the case with good flash fiction, I had to make sure every word, every line, every scene counted, and kept a constant eye on my overall word count as the stories progressed.

If you only write shorts—or only novels—I recommend trying the other format. Switching things up opens a whole new challenge and can teach you another skill set that can come in handy on your novels too.

And if you really want a challenge, try writing flash fiction—generally considered to be 1,000 words or less. It's a great crash course to learning what really counts in telling a story.

Remember, when we stop learning—when we decide we know it all as writers—is the day our writing starts to die.

WRITING WHAT YOU (DON'T) KNOW

They say you should write what you know.

I don't think that's really true—I write a lot of sci-fi and fantasy, and take readers places I have never been.

But sometimes I really do.

I was born in Southern California, and grew up in Tucson, Arizona. I've now spent a couple decades in my adopted hometown of Sacramento, California.

Sacramento was historically a bit of a "cow town." It's in the Central Valley, and although it's the state capital, it still thinks it's a small town. Since I've been here, though, it has grown and changed, slowly, sometimes imperceptibly. But changed nonetheless.

A few years back, I decided I wanted to write a serial tale for my blog, based on Sacramento. *The River City Chronicles* is full of places real and imagined in Sacramento, and experiences that native and transplanted Sacramentans will recognize. In this case, it really paid off to write what I know, because it gave the story a vibrancy and reality that's hard to fake.

Other times, though, this idea of only writing the things you are familiar with can be very limiting, especially as a writer of sci-fi and fantasy fiction.

One of the ways I set out to break this idea down is by writing characters who are not at all like me. One of my novels put me far out on three different limbs at once.

First, I had a deaf character, so I had to take great care to portray them responsibly, realize when I am violating the character by writing about things they couldn't possibly perceive, such as certain sounds (or conversely, when I forgot that a heavy sound might easily be "felt," if not heard), and had to make it clear to my readers when the character was communicating by voice, by sign language, by paper, and via mind to mind (this *is* sci-fi, after all).

I also had a non-binary character in this story. My brain has been wired by society from birth to think of gender as binary—male/female. So although the character was non-binary, my brain continued to substitute female pronouns for their chosen *se* and *ser*. I also had to try to get into ser head, and to see the world as se would see it, all the time not making a big deal about ser non-binary status. It was a lot for my old writer brain.

I also had two Black characters in the story. I tried to be clear about their race identity upfront. But even here, it was easy to go overboard, calling out skin color in the name of diversity for Black characters, but neglecting to do so when the characters were white.

I had beta/sensitivity readers for my deaf and non-binary characters (more on these later), though not specifically for the Black characters in the story. My betas helped me avoid doing injustices to both the characters and their communities.

My point is that you often do have to write what you don't know, and there's honor and adventure in the attempt.

When we go beyond our comfort zone to write characters who are very different from ourselves, we're going to make some mistakes. I don't think I've made any egregious ones, but I have been caught in a few.

It's *okay* to make mistakes. We all do it. Be respectful. Do your homework. And if someone calls you on something that they know better than you, accept what they have to tell you and act accordingly.

So go ahead. Stretch yourself. Write about a place, or a character, or an event you are not comfortable with, and see where it takes you.

It's one way to grow as a writer.

PLANTSING

I t's an age-old debate. Plotter or pantser? Is one better than the other? Which one are you?

A *plotter* is someone who plans out their entire story in advance. Plotters are known for making extensive outlines, doing deep dives into internet searches to pull together all the materials they will need, and making sure all their i's are dotted and t's are crossed before writing a word of the actual story. They are perfectionists, lovers of story arcs marked with specific "beats" that they plan to hit at exact points of the narrative to ensure their characters and plots reach the right highs and lows at the perfect time. We all know people like this in real life—folks who organize their lives via spreadsheets and calendar apps, who love to go with the flow, as long as the flow starts at 5:01 PM and wraps up punctually at seven, and not a minute later.

A *pantser*, on the other hand, is the free spirit of writing. Pantsers eschew anything in the way of advance planning for their stories, beyond maybe a general idea of a plot or an image of a really cool character. Pantsers love to explore while they're writing, and they don't like to be told what to do. To your average pantser, creating an outline is torture. It means they've already written the story, and it dulls their sense of adventure. In the real world, these are your friends who will take off on vacation on a whim, who love spending the day (and often far into the night) exploring a new city without a map, and are always trying strange new things, like mixing salsa, vanilla ice cream and Circus Peanuts (the candy, not the actual nuts).

Yes, that's a very specific example, and I did try it once. Spoiler alert, it was awful, but I'm not sorry.

So which should you be? Plotter or pantser? It comes down to personal preference.

When I first started writing, I was a total pantser. I'd just open a blank document and start typing, and then see where the writing winds led me.

But the winds of writing are a fickle thing. I ended up, more often than not, with a story only a few scenes long, and no idea where to take the story from there. To this day, I have a folder of what I now call "story starters"—never-finished pantser tales three or five pages long. I occasionally review them and choose one to pluck out and make into a whole story.

When pantsing failed me, I tried being a plotter. I wrote out a detailed outline for my story, hitting all of my desired plot points, right up to the beautifully crafted idea for the ending. And writing it felt like Groundhog Day, mirthlessly retracing the path I had already taken with my outline.

So I'd like to propose a third option—being a *plantser*.

Plantsing combines the best of both worlds. Basically, you create a very loose outline of where the story might go. I usually do this in a series of single lines in a Word document:

- Bartholomew the farm boy (we'll call him Bart) wakes up to find that the world has changed, and that magic is suddenly everywhere.
- Bart's sister Tessalia (we'll call her Tess) discovers she has a special (and very particular) magical power—she can make cows appear wherever she wants to.
- Bart and Tess set out together to find the origin of their powers, and why Bart doesn't seem to have one
- Bart and Tess meet a strange man on the way.

- Bart and Tess arrive in the newly magical city of Chicago, and run into many people who want to exploit her special power, including the head of Acme Meat Products.
- We find out that this is just before the fire that burned the city down, and Tess summons Mrs. O'Leary's cow moments before it starts the deadly blaze, saving the city. And we finally discover Bart's secret power, which is…

And yes, I'm aware that the whole "cow started the fire" thing was almost certainly a journalist's invention. It's fiction. Go with it.

And see what I did there, at the end? I left myself some wiggle room for my writer brain to play with. Maybe Bart can see the future, five minutes ahead of time, and he's the one who tells Tess to move the cow. Or maybe I'll come up with something better over the course of writing the story.

Overall, my outline is loose enough that it gives me some room to roam and explore while I'm writing.

What if they go on a side adventure that explains where their powers come from? What if the man turns out to be stage and screen actor Tim Curry, who has travelled back in time when everyone assumed he had just died? What if the fire happens anyway, because Tess teleports the wrong cow out of dear old Mrs. O'Leary's barn?

My point here is that having a loose outline *and* a goal for the end of the story helps you keep moving forward without hitting that brick wall of "I have no idea where this is going." It also makes it easy to follow your writer heart and make changes to the story on the fly, keeping the story fresh for you and your readers.

Does the writing take a sudden left turn? All you have to do is make a few changes to your loose outline, and *boom*, you're moving again.

In the end, it's up to you to decide which writing style serves you best. I know folks who thrive on building the world and figuring out the story in advance, and still have a blast writing it. And others for whom writing *anything* down in advance is a total anathema and stalls out their writer brain.

So give it a try, and see which one feels right to you. And just remember, there's no right or wrong way to write.

WRITING IN FIRST PERSON

When crafting a story, every writer has to make some key choices about what the story will be and where it will go:

- What's the genre?
- What's the tone?
- How about the setting?
- Who are the characters, and what's going to happen to them?
- How will they react?
- And will it all end?

But there's another choice we all make, consciously or unconsciously, that can have a huge impact on the story and how it's perceived by the reader:

Choosing the person you'll tell your story in, and the tense.

Most stories are told in third-person, simple past:

Someone knocked on the door. Zippy the dingo went to open it, but he had no hands, so he waited patiently for it to swing open of its own accord.

Third-person is handy because it lets us swing the camera all around our protagonist(s), showing things that might not be noticed if filtered through a more restrictive point of view, like second or first. But we'll come back to third-person in the next chapter.

Many authors prefer using first-person. Let's revisit that little snippet from above about Zippy the dingo, but switched to first person:

> *Someone knocked at the door. I perked up my ears and raced to it, then sat down on my haunches, staring at the knob in despair. I have no hands. Resigned, I waited on my dingo paws and butt for whoever was on the other side to open it.*

First-person is much more restrictive than third-person, in that you can only convey things the character sees/feels/etc. themselves. But it's also more intimate, letting us slip past that wall that separates reader and character. The reader gets to *be* the character for a bit, to experience the world as they do.

And while third-person lends itself well to multiple point of view character casts, first-person often works best for single POV tales, although that's not a hard and fast rule. If you plan to write multiple first-person POVs in a single story, it's important to set up a clear structure (like alternating chapters between POVs) and to develop a distinct *voice* for each different first-person POV character in your story.

You also need to be careful with how far you stretch the character's perception. For folks who normally write in third-person, it's distressingly easy to slip in details that the character couldn't possibly know or perceive.

It gets easier with practice, and writing a first-person narrative can also be a much more intimate experience for the writer.

Most first-person tales are told in simple past tense, like most third-person stories. But you can up the immediacy of your story by putting it in the present tense too, so that all the action is not only happening to the reader in the first-person driver's seat, but it's also happening *now*.

> *Someone's knocking at the door. I perk up my ears and race to it, then sit down on my haunches, staring at the knob in despair. I have no hands.*

Resigned, I wait on my dingo paws and butt for whoever is on the other side to open it.

My best analogy for this is a movie I saw half a lifetime ago in a crowded theater. I don't remember the name anymore. But I do remember sitting in the front row because all the other seats were taken. And I vividly recall being *right there* as a car barreled across an empty field, almost into my lap. It was a thrill ride, a rush I'd never get from viewing the scene from the top row.

For one of my recent short stories, first-person seemed like an ideal fit. It's about assuming another identity, and putting the reader right there in the character's head as things suddenly go wrong, really helped me to increase the tension. I initially wrote it in first-person simple past, but when I decided to snip out bits of time as the character fades in and out of awareness, present tense seemed to work even better to convey the immediacy of his disorientation.

Never written a first-person or present tense narrative? Try it and see if you like it for one of your stories. It can be fun to convert a third-person story to first-person, and see how it shifts the whole feel of the work.

In general, I tend to favor first-person more for short stories than for novellas, but that's just my personal taste. I've seen it done well both ways.

What about using other tenses besides present and simple past? I've never seen a story written in simple future, future perfect, or past perfect. They'd sound really weird to me, but who knows? Maybe there's an author and a story out there that could make them into something amazing.

For now, I'm sticking with first-person, past or present tense.

Until I *will have changed* my mind.

WRITING IN THIRD PERSON

I n the last chapter, we talked about writing in *first-person*. But what about the more common *third-person* usage?

Third-person means using he/she/they/etc. pronouns—stories that describe the action from outside the characters. It comes in three basic flavors:

Third Person Omniscient: The most common of the three. Omniscient allows you to have multiple viewpoint characters, and an outside "omniscient" narrator who's basically describing the story as it goes (i.e., you). This version of third-person gives you the most freedom, as you can *head hop* (although doing so within a scene is strongly discouraged) and move around your story's playing field at will. You can also dive into the characters' heads to show us what they are thinking and feeling. This is what I write the majority of my stories in.

Third Person Objective: This is similar to omniscient but reports the story objectively without giving the reader a window on the characters' thoughts and feelings. You can still head hop and give a wider picture, but this version tends to feel drier and less rich in the telling. Generally speaking, it's more suited to non-fiction reporting than vivid fiction prose.

Third Person Limited: This is the most intimate of the versions, and also (as its name suggests) the most limited. The narrator (you) only has a window into a single character's thoughts, feelings, and perceptions. If that character doesn't know something, the author (and by extension, the reader) doesn't either. I most commonly use this in short stories, but you can also make an entire novel out of it. You'll just need to come up with some creative ways to get your character the information they need during the story—without becoming a writing contortionist.

So why use third-person instead of first-person?

Third-person is what the majority of stories are told in. It's comfortable and establishes a small amount of distance between the story and the reader.

If reading first-person is like sitting in the front row of the movie theater as a car comes crashing at you at 100 MPH, third-person is sitting in the back row with the best view *and* a big tub of hot buttered popcorn.

Third-person, in all its forms, also gives you a little more leeway to take note of the world around your characters. In first-person:

I walked into the room. It was small, with some kind of wood trim, and a neat wooden desk in the middle. Seeing natural wood again made me happy.

In third-person, you can share a bit more than the character knows, although you don't want to overdo it and info-dump:

Alex walked into the room. The walls were paneled in a rich, hand-stained oak, while the small desk in the center was mahogany, its surface polished to a deep sheen. It made Alex smile to see natural wood again, warmth spreading through their chest.

Third Limited is similar to the first-person example above, in that you can't know anything beyond what your character knows:

Alex walked into the room. It was small, with some kind of wood trim, and a neat wooden desk in the middle. It's good to see natural wood again.

And Third Objective strips out a lot of the beauty and joy:

Alex walked into the room. It was small, with oak trim, and a neat wooden desk in the middle.

There are good reasons to use each of these, mostly driven by the kind of story you want to tell and how you want to convey information to your reader. Whichever version of third-person you choose, just be sure to be consistent. Each version has a different feel/purpose, and putting them all together can make a story feel jumbled and disjointed.

But if you do choose to mix them, go for it—experimentation is part of the whole writer thing, after all! But know why you're doing it.

Like they say, know the rule before you break it.

PART THREE
DIVING IN

So you've got a good idea what you want to write about, and all of your writerly tools and skills at the ready. What now? I have some thoughts...

A LITTLE PHILOSOPHY: IMMERSE YOURSELF IN YOUR NEW WORLD

One of the things fiction writers yearn for is those moments when we become totally immersed in one of our stories, when the writing just flows out of our fingers as if we were tapping into another world, simply conduits for the stories that are already there, waiting to be told.

When I get deep into one of my sci-fi stories, I start to practically live in that other world. It's not uncommon for me to write a couple thousand words a day, and the story and its characters are on constant rotation in my head. My subconscious gathers little details in our own world that I realize I need to account for in my tale.

Does this future version of our world still have religion? How has it changed over the years? Is it more like Buddhism or Catholicism? What do they think is a sin?

What about food—how is it different from ours? How is it the same?

What's the driving ethos in their society? Are they a democracy? A meritocracy? An authoritarian state?

How are their names chosen? Are they like ours, and if not, why not?

How are their children raised?

Each day brings new ideas, new revelations, new pieces of the puzzle.

Some of them go right into the story. Some go into the editing notes for my second draft. And some go into the hopper in my head to spin, and maybe bear fruit somewhere down the line.

The characters, too, are on a spin cycle in my head. When I first start a new story, I begin with a general idea of each one. But over time, as I write their stories and let them stew in my head, they become clearer and clearer. What they look like, how they act. How they react. The things that formed them and their world view.

At different times during the day, I close my eyes and imagine the world. I could actually see the city of Redemption in its lava tube on the moon, its light wells letting in sunlight, its wide boulevards lit by bioluminescent trees.

I could feel the wind roaring past the moon jumper, carrying my intrepid team of dropnauts tumbling toward the Earth.

And I could see the mural Rosemary's mother painted in the hall in the Preserve, in all its vibrant diversity and color.

Each time there are more details, a story told over and over that becomes richer with every pass.

Immerse yourself in your world. Live it and breathe it, taste its flavors, and savor its colors until it becomes as real to you as your own.

Then your readers will be able to sink into it too.

DIVING INTO YOUR CHARACTERS

Writing fascinating, well-rounded characters comes easily to some people. Character traits, past histories, and quirky, unique personalities seem to just flow out of their fingers and onto the page, and every book is a new adventure filled with a fascinating cast.

I am *not* one of those people. If you are, you can stop reading here.

I grew up devouring science-fiction and fantasy, and I was hooked on the *Big Concept*. Dragons are real and can travel *between* in the blink of an eye? OMG, give me that book.

Living spaceships will carry humanity across the stars? I am so there for it.

Giant sandworms that will eat you alive just for walking across the sand? Here, take my money.

And yes, some of these *concept* writers were also great with characterization. But even if they weren't, it didn't matter to me. I was oblivious, flying halfway across the galaxy with my arms flung wide on a life-changing adventure.

When I finally got serious about writing. I had *concepts* in spades—broken worlds, generation ships, astronauts, and werewolves. And sometimes even astronauts with werewolves.

But one of the consistent criticisms I got in those first few years was that my characters fell a little flat. No one said they were horrible, but they just didn't spring to life off the page. And so began my journey to be a better character writer.

I tried a number of things, the first of which was simply paying more attention to my characters—who they are, where they come from, and what they want.

I've read books, worked up formulas, and made long lists of character traits and possessions.

In the end, it all came down to one thing. Knowing down to my bones who my characters are.

So here's the process I've come up with to build scintillating characters from the ground up:

What Are the Basics?: I still start with a list. I know, it's all dry, basic stuff, and maybe not so helpful in building the actual tone of the character. But it helps me get a sense of where they came from, what formed them, what they look like, and maybe a quirk or tic or two I can use to help set them apart from the others. And it's a great reference for when I need to remember who had blue eyes, who had a mohawk, and who scratches their armpits whenever they get nervous. Sometimes I do this at the get-go. Other times I let it grow organically as I make my way through the story.

Where Did You Come From?: For each of my characters, I come up with a backstory. What events molded them, making them who they are today? Were any of those events intersectional with the other characters in the story? What was the result? I'll go into this in more depth in the next chapter.

What Drives You?: I assign a primary motivation to each character, often in the form of a verb/action. Run away. Double down. Pass the buck. Something that describes their go-to move when things get hard. I learned this at a book convention (see the "Preparing for the Con" chapter in the Groups and Events section later in this book for more about cons), and it's been an invaluable tool for short-handing my characters' motivations. In one of my books, a character lost his mother at an early age in a tragic fire, and was scared to death of losing someone else, so he *ran away* from anything good. His love interest was a guard who needed to *save and protect* everyone he loved, and was frustrated when his crush kept finding ways to keep things cool between them. *Run Away* is inherently in conflict with *Save and Protect*. Setting up actions that conflict with one another is a great way to build drama between your characters.

What Are You Afraid Of?: I also try to figure out my characters' greatest fears—what would absolutely gut them if it happened to them? Dangle this in front of them and watch them squirm. I picked this one up from *The Art of Character*, by David Corbett.

How Are You All Tangled Up With the Others?: Then I figure out the interpersonal relationships with the other primary character(s). What do they want from each other? Where is there conflict? This is especially helpful when constructing scenes—knowing what each character is after when they start, and what happens if/when they get it (or not).

What Little Things Make You *You*?: In addition to the characters' physical characteristics (hair color, eyes, height, skin tone, etc.). I think about the little habits each character displays that make them unique. One of my favorite examples of this is Nynaeve in the Wheel of Time series, who is always yanking on her braid when she's in distress. It makes her unique—she has a braid (visual detail) and she pulls on it, creating an action which reminds us that she's in a near constant state of agitation over something or other.

What's Your Character Trope?: For this, I've drawn heavily on Amy Lane's *Crafting Category Romance*. Although technically a book about writing romance, Lane nails it with her character tropes, which can be used in almost any fictional genre. Each of them comes with built-in conflicts that can help drive the story. For one of my recent books, I chose Fish Out of Water and Orphan for one of the primary characters, and

Protector for the other, a trait which gets exploited (as you do) and turned on its head by the end of the story.

What TV/Movie Character Are You?: Part of the art of writing good characters is visualizing all of this and carrying it in your head as you write each scene. Where is the character coming from? How will they react to the influences in that scene? And how will other characters react to them? For this, I find it helpful at times to identify a character or relationship from a favorite series or movie of mine that fit the characters. For one book, I used the relationship between Emily and Lorelei Gilmore in *The Gilmore Girls* as a template for a mother-daughter pair in the story —even though it's a sci-fantasy set on a planet far away in space and time from Hartford, Connecticut. It's the relationship dynamic that counts, not the character details. If you took away all the sci-fantasy settings, you could probably picture most conversations between these two taking place over a fine meal in Emily Gilmore's posh dining room.

Let Me Into Your Head: Another useful tool is this writing exercise—put your character into various situations and see how they will act/react. I used this extensively with a character in one of my recent novels, and it really helped me with my primary character—who he was, how he felt, and how he would respond to various situations and pressures. My favorite book for this is *Write Characters Your Readers Won't Forget* by Stant Litore, which is chock-full of practical writing exercises to take you on a deep dive into your characters.

Just Write: The final piece of advice I'll give you is to just dive in. You've done the prep work, and you have your notes to fall back on. But just like you'll probably never be fluent in a foreign language until you spend some time in a country where it's spoken, you won't really know your characters until you immerse yourself in your story and start to write them.

So talk to your characters. Wine and dine them, and get to know who they really are.

They may surprise you. Despite all of your careful planning, they may exhibit traits you didn't expect, or push back on the assumptions you've made about them. That's okay… the longer you work with them, the more clearly they will speak in your head.

When you truly understand them, you can begin to write them as the magnificent, unique beasts that they are, and bring them to life for your readers.

That's part of the magic of writing.

DAMAGE

"What's your damage, Heather?"

We all carry damage around with us in some way, shape, or form, like an unwanted hitchhiker. Damage from things that were done to us as children. Damage from things we did to others. Damage from the world and society at large.

I carry the damage of homophobia. Of being called the *f* word and *queer* and a *sissy*, damage from the nasty looks other kids gave me when I was a teenager. I carry the damage of shattered hopes, dreams, and expectations, and the damage of a few hundred writing rejections that feed my imposter syndrome (but that's a story for another chapter).

In real life people, damage causes great harm. It can shape and channel our lives, and if unchecked, it can ruin us.

In fictional characters, a little damage can make things far more interesting. Consider:

Riane has wanted to be a starship captain their entire life. They worked hard, studied hard, got into a good school, and by twenty-two, were chosen by the UAS for their elite star ship captain training school at

Moonbase Alpha. They became a captain at twenty-five, and their family was immensely proud of them.

Warm and fuzzy and heartwarming. And as my husband Mark often points out, happy, well-adjusted characters can also be boring as hell.
So how about this instead?

Riane was abandoned at an orphanage at the age of twelve, told by their mother that they would never amount to anything. It created a deep-seated mistrust of family and authority, something they would never entirely outgrow.

Passing through a series of foster homes, they learned to be self-sufficient. They also vowed to prove their mother wrong.

They got into the UAS on a hardship scholarship, but were almost thrown out because of their regular run-ins with teachers at the school, who Riane thought were all too cautious and less intelligent than they were.

But Riane's fast thinking and willingness to do what everyone told them not to saved half the school when a rogue ship engine almost blew it to bits, and only their quick action against orders stopped it in time.

Still, they were thrown out of school for disobeying the school authorities, and ended up signing on for scut work on a cross-system hauler. When they finally rose to the role of captain on their own merit, with the respect of their crew mates, they sent a six-word message to their mother, now living on a meager pension in Queens. "What do you think of me now?"

This Riane is much more interesting, with fault lines to explore (and exploit). These can become both motivations and self-imposed blockades that your characters must find a way to overcome.
Maybe they drink because of something their uncle did to them when

they were three, and your story is about learning to find the light again (and spaceships, of course).

Maybe they broke up with someone who was dying, and have lived with the guilt for three years, culminating with the receipt of a funeral invitation for that person. On Mars.

Here's a little exercise. Think of your own close friends and family, people you know very well. Was there a tragic event or hard decision in one of their pasts that shaped the course of their life? Something that dictates, even now, how they approach their lives and future decisions?

For my grandmother Hazel, it was the Great Depression. She learned to live with very little, and saved anything that might be useful later. She also learned to be generous and give whatever she could to whomever needed it.

Now take a character from your current work in progress, and give them a similar trauma. How would it make them act/react differently in your story? What if Markey was born on Vega Seven just after they lost contact with Earth, thrusting the planet and its economy into a horrific spiral from which it took two decades to climb out of? What did that do to young Markey's psyche? What scars does she still carry from it, as she looks up at the stars, and tries to imagine a distant Earth?

In one of my books, as mentioned before, a character's mother was killed right in front of him in a horrific fire when he was a child. Now he's none too thrilled with fire, of course, but on a deeper level, he is afraid to let anyone in, because they might leave him at any time. He chooses to be a thief, an occupation where he can have minimal contact with others and take back something to help fill the void of what he lost. He turns away his dearest friend (who wants more from him) because he can't bear to lose him. And he overcompensates by giving some of his ill-gotten goods to the poorest of the poor.

His damage has shaped his life in ways which I continue to play with throughout the story.

So find your character's damage. What was it? When did it happen? How did your character react? And how does it shape them, even now? Will they overcome it, use it to further their own ends, or will it destroy them in the end?

Then you've got a story.

BUILDING A WORLD

So you want to build a world. How do you go about it?

I'm a sci-fi writer, so I love the big concept. I usually start with an overarching feature that makes the world interesting to me, and hopefully to my readers as well. In one of my books, it was the concept of a broken world—a half-sphere hanging against the inky blackness of space.

In another it was a man-made cylindrical world that arches up all around the reader, almost claustrophobic in its embrace, especially for those who grew up under Earth's open sky.

And in a third, it was the surprise about how two worlds were connected.

But as they say, the devil's in the details. Once you get down to ground level in any of these stories, you have to start building your world from scratch, one that will feel both familiar and tantalizingly exotic to the reader. Throw in too much alienness and it becomes a struggle for the reader to relate. Make it too mundane, and the reader will be bored.

Some of my friends are like sculptors. They write ungodly-long stories, and then slice and dice them, removing scenes surgically, working like Michelangelo to reveal the sleek sculpture hidden beneath layers of marble.

I'm an additive writer—more like a painter. I start with a basic idea of the world itself—how it works, what it looks like from 30,000 feet. As I write the first draft, I start to sketch in the details, sort of a pencil version of how the world looks, what it smells like, and how it feels.

I often make actual sketches too—maps, room layouts, etc.—to help me visualize the setting and the action.

Over the course of several more drafts, I add in more details, mixing common things you're familiar with in slightly new ways—box corn, for instance, a genetically modified square-shaped corn; or the poor swamp bear who stares up forlornly at our party from the midst of a flood.

Each brush stroke adds a little more color, until the final work—assuming I've done my job right—feels both complete and immersive.

I love analyzing the world building in the stories I read, especially sci-fi and fantasy. But I've had to learn to minimize the data dumps—those bits where an author spends a page (or three) describing in minute detail the way their special world works.

I still remember reading one historical fantasy where the author spent almost thirty pages cataloging her knowledge of ancient herbal lore. Impressive, sure, but a real momentum killer.

To be most effective, good world-building needs to happen within the confines of the action of the story—slip it in so that you barely notice the craft of it.

Once you can manage that, your worlds will shine.

DETAILS MATTER

Have you ever seen the movie *Somewhere in Time*? It featured Christopher Reeve in a heartbreaking time traveler's tale.

Reeve's character found a way to go back in time by surrounding himself entirely with objects from the past, and then willing himself back to their period. But the illusion had to be perfect.

And in so doing, he met the love of his life.

His undoing? A single, modern penny, forgotten in his pants pocket, that ultimately shattered that illusion and sent him back to his own time.

Writing can be a bit like that, especially when you write stories about the past or future.

We all know the present well enough, but throw one bad detail into a historical tale—your Knight of the Round Table uttering the word "cool," or your Victorian seamstress driving home in her Hyundai Sonata, and you've lost your audience.

Although, in the right hands, that could be a really cool story.

The same thing is true about writing the future, and sci-fi readers are especially picky about getting all the details right. Is your character in 2050 still using an iPad? Are your 25th century teens on TikTok? Is your main character three hundred years hence named Brittney or Courtney?

Every detail of your story has to be forward-thinking and blend in with your future world. Seamless. Any misplaced details will stick out like a modern penny.

It's hard seeing the future. We are all products of our time, and writing good sci-fi means questioning *everything* in your story. It can be exhausting (this is where a good developmental editor comes in handy), but when you pull it off, the results can be amazing.

So mind the details, and if you do it right, the result will feel authentic through and through.

PROCRASTINATION AND CHOCOLATE

I am a master procrastinator. As a writer, that probably goes without saying. I can put something off for days and weeks at a time, through a variety of creative methods.

These are among my many excuses and diversions (and a frightening peek at how my brain works when it's time to write):

- I just don't feel like it
- I haven't figured out the next scene
- I have laundry to do
- When was the last time I clipped my toenails?
- I got so much writing done yesterday—I deserve a break
- I'm hungry. Think I will go get something to eat
- Is the mail here yet?
- Oooh, look something cool on Facebook
- I really, really need to re-alphabetize the spice drawer
- I do have a "real" job, you know
- I'm a horrible writer. Why even bother?
- Did I turn off the teakettle this morning?
- Maybe it's time to clip my toenails again.

Procrastination really *is* an art, when you think about it. As writers, we have the gift of putting off the one thing we love and hate most—writing.

Plus there's the whole "my desk is so boring—I work here all day long" thing—do I really want to write in the same place I do my emails, accounting, and business calls?

So I have devised a new strategy. It's nothing earth-shattering or even particularly novel (see what I did there? "Novel!" I kill myself!).

I alter my environment. When it's time to write, I turn off the overhead light, open the blinds to let in a little natural sunlight, and put in my headphones with the music cranked up high. I might even grab a blanket now and then to wrap around myself for that snuggly feeling. The idea is to change my space so it doesn't feel like I'm working.

But the key ingredient here, the thing that makes it all come together, is chocolate.

I've always been a sucker for chocolate, especially dark chocolate. It has fewer calories than milk chocolate and less sugar, and anti-oxidants that are good for my little writer heart.

I take a square of my favorite chocolate and break it into a bunch of little pieces, and then work on a reward system. Finish a page, get a piece of chocolate. My chocolate reward encourages me to stay put and write.

One other thing I do, on those days when I feel sluggish, is to get up and do fifty jumping jacks. It puts a little oxygen in your bloodstream and wakes up your brain. Then it's back to chocolate and writing.

Anyone can do this. And it doesn't have to be chocolate. If you absolutely love carrots, make it carrots. If you are cuckoo for Cocoa Puffs, make it Cocoa Puffs. Maybe peppermint candy is your thing. Whatever feels like a reward to you and will keep you at the keyboard.

And then…

Take a deep breath. Clear your head. Chant "I am a good writer, or at least I don't suck" ten times to yourself.

Then sit down at the keyboard and write.

WRITER'S WAIT

They call it writer's block. I never liked the term. It suggests all those words are stuck inside your head somewhere, just waiting to burst out if you can figure out how to free the blockage.

I spent three weeks agonizing over the plot for the last book in one of my trilogies. I was dealing with eight major characters, trying to deliver on the romance piece for a third time, and planning to wrap up all of the loose ends by the end of the book.

I sat down to outline things on a couple of occasions, and nothing felt quite right. It was like trying to stuff yourself into a pair of jeans that's three sizes too small–it felt forced, and the story just sat there on the page, taunting me.

Then I had a bit of a revelation on how to lay things out in a more organic way, and suddenly I was ready to write.

Instead of writer's block, I like to call it writer's *wait*. Whenever I have a hard time moving forward with a story, it usually means there's something wrong with it, something I am too close to it to see. I'm trying to force it in a direction it doesn't want to go.

And so I've learned to wait it out, working on other things, to give my brain a chance to sort things out. Sometimes you need a way to move through the resistance and figure out what's really wrong.

If you've never read it, I'd like to recommend a fantastic book that every writer should have. It's called *Writing Down the Bones*, short meditations on writing and exercises for writers, by Natalie Goldberg. It was first published in 1986, but it's timeless. Seriously, get this book and stick it in your bathroom. The chapters are all short reads, perfect for those few minutes you typically have to yourself a few times a day.

One of my favorite exercises in the book is deceptively simple—timed writing. It's something Ken Macrorie also advocated for in *Telling Writing*.

We're not talking about writing anything structured—a story, a poem, or an essay. Just sitting down with a notebook and a pad of paper, setting a timer, and then writing whatever comes out of your head.

When you are stuck on a story, or blocked by fear or pain or heartache, give yourself permission to write without a roadmap.

While I love Ms. Goldberg's idea of using an actual pen and paper—being connected so viscerally to the art of writing—I'm not wedded to this romantic view of the craft. To me, the most important thing is that you write, not how you choose to do it.

Goldberg likens this exercise to running. You let your mind run a bit every day, and slowly you tone your writing muscles, getting better and better at this whole *words* thing.

So try this. When you're feeling blocked, pull out a pad of paper or open a new file on your writing device. Set your timer for five minutes to start. Then just write.

Let go of all your preconceived notions of what you *should* be writing or how to do it. Just put down whatever comes out—let the words flow. You're not a careful weigher of ideas today. Instead you're an Olympic runner, and you have a pack of ravenous, snarling mountain lions at your back.

Write like your life depends on it, and don't stop until your timer buzzes. Then sit back and take a deep breath.

Congratulations. You just broke through your wall.

Every time you write—whether it's a novel, a poem, or a bunch of words hurled out onto a page—you are honing your craft, whether you're writing something structured or just writing to stretch out your limbs.

So write like the hellhounds are coming for your soul.

And don't let that wall keep you away from what you were meant to do.

THE "HOLY SHIT" MOMENT

S peaking of immersion, sometimes when you are deep into a story, something amazing happens. Every writer who has been doing this gig for a while has probably experienced something like this:

A character suddenly reveals something about themselves that you'd never guessed when you first created them.

Or maybe what was just a minor throw-away plot point or description suddenly blossoms and veers the story off onto a whole new course.

Or that guy you mentioned way back in book one suddenly wants his own plot arc in book three.

As a writer, I *live* for those moments—when the writing feels alive, when it practically *sings* under my hands on the keyboard.

I often find myself feeling a sense of deja vu when I'm writing—I mean, how many times can you write a "walking through the woods" scene and make it *fresh* and *new*?

And about halfway through, Jimmy having lunch at the diner starts to feel *a lot* like that time when Christian had lunch at the fast-food place. Writers tend to fall into patterns with our work—after all, the source is always the same, our own lives and experiences. Writing similar things over and over again becomes dull and repetitive, and the reader feels it too.

But sometimes the writing takes on a life of its own. It's like riding a tiger. You dig your hands into the fur at the scruff of its neck and hold on for dear life, and hope it doesn't turn and bite you. And you have as little idea where it's all going as your reader.

At their worst, these moments can totally derail your story, leaving you lost in the weeds with a hungry tiger.

But at their best, they can imbue your story with a sense of surprise and wonder—a how-the-hell-did-we-get-here moment—that is as rewarding for you as it is for the reader.

I had one of those moments in one of my short stories. The smallest story description, planted in the first few pages, literally blossomed overnight and carried me into the most important part of the climactic ending, and set the stage for an entire trilogy later on.

I call these Holy Shit Moments.

It's the flash in your writer brain when suddenly something connects with something else in your story, and your plot takes off like a rocket on a whole new direction. It's the Aha! moment, the flash of genius, the classic lightbulb-above-the-head thing.

They often come to me when I'm driving or riding my bike—when my writer brain has a little peace and quiet to work on unresolved issues. My writer brain likes peace. And quiet. And wheels, apparently.

And just like that, something clicks into place, a new idea that makes the whole story make sense, and imbues it with a new energy and direction.

When it happens for you, embrace it and ride it to wherever it takes you.

FACING DOWN A DEADLINE

You're an author. That comes with a certain number of built-in idiosyncrasies:

- You probably carry a notebook (or use a notes app) to jot down ideas "on the fly"
- Music is a font of story ideas for you, and you are often caught with a thoughtful expression on your face and your tongue between your teeth, contemplating the lyrics
- You have created a safe writer's cave where you can retreat and shut the door on the outside world
- You often go for days without a shower when you are deeply immersed in your work (don't worry—we'll cover this in the next chapter)

You are writer—hear you roar.

But there is one thing that has the power to strike fear in our little writer hearts: a looming deadline.

You see, as writers, we like to think of ourselves as free spirits, letting the winds of the words carry us where they may, free of all earthly constraints. But that flies out the window when we're faced with a due date.

So what's a poor writer to do?

Organization: Remember that old joke? Once you can fake that, you've got it made? Or maybe it was sincerity? In any case, this is, hands down, the most important thing you can do to meet an approaching deadline. It's simple. Count the number of writing days you have, divide the work you have to get done by that many days, and stick it on a calendar. There, you should be feeling better already, right? All you have to do is *HOLY MOTHER OF GOD*—write 15,000 words a day.

Set Up a Punishment/Reward System: Okay, so you've figured out that there is no way on this green Earth that you can get this damned project done on time. Still, it must be done. So you have to motivate yourself to actually do the work. There are a number of ways to do this.

You can get one of those apps that penalizes you for not finishing your writing task on time. Many of my writer friends prefer this method.

But if that doesn't do it for you, you can also reward yourself with an episode of your favorite TV show, but choose wisely. If your reward series only has a handful of episodes, you may run out of motivation too quickly.

As I mentioned earlier, I prefer my old standby—chocolate. And for punishment if you fail in your daily task? Give up something you really like for the day. If you don't trust yourself, leave it in the hands of a friend, spouse or other family member who will hold you to account.

Clear the Calendar: You can also free up time to meet your deadline by clearing unnecessary tasks from the calendar.

That dental cleaning? It can wait until next month. Who needs teeth anyway? Teeth don't write.

Grocery shopping? Oh come on. You can easily survive on that box of ramen in the garage for a few more days. Snack tip—it's delicious dry, and saves you the cooking time.

Paying the bills? Well, I gotta make money to spend money, right?

Do the Work: I know, we all wish the writing would just flow out of our fingers like custard from an eclair when you squeeze it hard (and yes, it *is* fun licking the chocolate off your fingers afterward). But the cold, hard reality is that writing isn't always like that. Hell, it's not like that most of the time. As writers, we just have to put our butts in the chair and grind it out sometimes.

But don't worry. You can always add the magic later.

Beg for More Time: If all else fails, you can go to your publisher, get on your hands and knees, and beg for more time. It's a sad fact of life, but writers are a notoriously unreliable species. Publishers know this, and are used to hearing this kind of request.

Just don't pull this one too often. It's a short hop from "happens all the time—not a big deal" to "this is happening all the time—you writers are a dime a dozen."

Don't be a dime.

REMEMBERING TO SHOWER

I f you're a writer and you're anything like me, well, first of all, I'm sorry.

You probably have a day job or three (commonly known as the Evil Day Job, or EDJ) and you madly scramble for bits of time to write, edit, feed your social media accounts, plot out your next novel, network, and self-promote in your overloaded schedule.

But you may be missing a few key things in your life. Things your significant other might have noticed too—the reason they wrinkle their nose every time you walk into the room.

This list may seem a little tongue-in-cheek, but it's also a serious reminder to engage with the world while you are working on your writing:

Remember to Shower. OK, so this is Hygiene 101, but many of us get so wrapped up in our work that we literally forget to hold ourselves to the minimum standards of human decency and presentability. Shower *at least* every three days. Put it on your calendar. Apply deodorant daily. Do what you do to present yourself in a professional way that will enhance your author brand. Unless your brand is "long-haired feral biker," in which case, as you were.

Eat Things That Are Not Pure Sugar. Yes, we all know how easy it is to slip into the trap of eating *power foods* to fuel your writing. Tons of chocolate. Chugging soda like a sugar athlete. But those "foods" will seriously mess up your brain if you don't counter them with some *actual* food. Eat a salad. Make yourself a bowl of fruit and granola. Heck, even a hamburger and fries are better than a steady diet of Wild Cherry Pepsi and Oreos. Well, *marginally* better.

Engage in Actual Human Conversation. Your writing needs more than sugar as fuel. It also needs your engaged brain. And nothing is more engaging than actually holding a conversation with someone else. Your spouse, your children, and your friends would probably enjoy actually hearing from you once in a while. Step out of your writer cave and see what they've been up to for the last 72 hours.

Leave the House. Yes, you have that deadline bearing down on you. Sure, you're feeling intense pressure to get it done. And your boss is demanding extra overtime hours for the Schnartzen-Diebowitz account. But there's also sunshine. Remember sunshine? The wonderful feeling of a warm breeze on your face? The chirping of birds in the trees? Get outside for a short walk. Clear your head and get a little exercise and give your writer brain some room to roam. It will make sitting in that chair for the next seventy-two hours a little more bearable.

In short, remember to be human. It's where you get all those experiences that will make your writing richer.

REDISCOVERING THE JOY

Sometimes we forget that we got into this whole writing gig because we *love* writing. No, not just love it. Need it, like an addict needs his fix. Most authors I know are not happy if they're not writing.

And yet, sometimes I'm not happy when I am, either.

There can be many reasons for this, including:

- The endless cycle of submissions and rejections, which can suck the soul right out of your body
- Your "evil day job" workload, which can keep you from concentrating on your writing as much as you'd like to
- Slogging through the muddy middle of a novel when everything seems derivative and you're sure you'll never reach the end

There are many more reasons we can lose the joy of writing, but regardless of the cause, it's important that we find a way to bring it back if we're going to keep doing this thing for the rest of our lives.

So it's time for a re-set. I thought I'd share the things I do to find the joy again when writing has become a dull, maddening, rote exercise.

Change Your Routine: Sometimes we get too settled into our regular writing habits. We always write at 2 PM in the coffee shop down the street, on the same laptop we've been using for five years, drinking a mocha latte. So why not shake it up? Try writing at home at 3 AM in your underwear when you get up to go pee—I know, I said before that a regular writing time is best. But work with me. We're shaking things up here.

Take your phone to the park, and write a scene in an email on your phone and send it to yourself. Or write a little something on a napkin while you're enjoying the better part of a bag of Oreos in your kitchen. It's not about changing your habits for the rest of your life. You're just pulling your writer brain out of its rut and giving it a new mode to explore.

Write Freeform: This is a great exercise, and can also be really helpful if you're blocked in a particular project. Just sit down wherever you normally work, set a timer for five or ten minutes, and write whatever comes out of your head. Stream of consciousness gibberish. Shopping lists. A hundred words starting with "q." Observations on the latest episode of that streaming show you're obsessed with. The only rule is that you can't stop writing until the timer goes off. This kind of free-flowing expression helps free you from your inner critic—what's there to criticize? And it works out your writing muscles too.

Take a Writing Sabbatical: Sometimes your writer brain starts overheating, and that's not fun for either of you. Just like anything else, we often push ourselves too hard to write when our mind requires a little relaxation or diversion. So take a three-day writing break. Play a video game, eat some ice cream, and lie in the hammock (if you have one) under a shady tree in the afternoon heat. Let your unconscious mind work on what's not right in your story, and when you go back to writing again, you'll be better equipped to fix it.

Read a Book or Watch a Film: Writer brains are great at taking in information and filing it away in your head, ready to spit it out onto the page in new combinations. But you need to feed that brain. Find a good book in your genre, or a movie that fires you up. As you're reading/watching, think about what makes the story work for you, or what doesn't. Take it apart in your head and figure out how it made you feel the way it did. Let your brain soak up the ideas like a squirrel storing nuts for a cold winter.

Switch Gears: If you're not feeling the writing love for your current WIP, set it aside and work on something completely different. I often use this time to write a short story that's in a whole different genre than my work in progress. It gives me something new to sink my teeth into, and leaves me fresh to return to my original story when I'm done.

Remind Yourself Why You Love The Story: When we start a new book, we're in the honeymoon period. We picture ourselves happy together, exchange love letters, and pretend the future will never bring us sadness. Then somewhere in the muddy middle, we sink into depression as our inner critics do their work. When it becomes debilitating, it's often worth rereading your WIP from the start to help you remember how much you loved it then—what magic made it light up for you. Sometimes you'll even discover where it went off track, and set off in a brand-new, better direction.

Writing isn't always fun—if it was, everyone would do it. Sometimes we do have to just power through, especially through the muddy middle.

But it shouldn't always be hard or joyless either. It's those writing highs that we all live for, after all—when it all *clicks* and the writing just flows.

So when you're feeling down, try something new to shake things up a bit.

Find a way back to your writing joy.

PART FOUR
TRICKS AND TIPS

Sometimes we need a little something to jumpstart the plot, a little writer grease to keep the engine humming. In this section, I'll share a few tools and ideas to help you do just that.

A LITTLE PHILOSOPHY: THE POWER OF DOWNTIME

Everyone needs downtime. Even writers. I know this, and yet I am spectacularly bad at actually letting myself enjoy it.

Writer brains, as any writer will attest, are strange things. Mine is a magpie, flitting through life and chasing whatever is bright, shiny, and new.

One day, we had lunch with friends. One of them comes from a family of "K's"—every sibling's first name starts with "K." And then she mentioned that one of their daughter's names started with an "E."

And off my little writer brain went.

Families with kids whose names start with the same letter > a child whose name starts with a different one > I wonder if most families like that purposely name their kids with another starting letter > I knew another family like that > their names all started with D > Damon, my high school boyfriend, was one of them > My mother was walking her dogs the other day and ran into someone who asked if she was Scott's mother. It was one of Damon's brothers > What a small world we live in.

Note that my final destination wasn't anywhere near where I started.

And keep in mind this whole thing took less than three seconds to go through my head.

My writer brain loves to wander and explore the connections between things.

And yet, when I am writing, I set word count goals to meet, whether I am inspired or not. I am an evil taskmaster. So what's a poor writer brain to do?

If you're a writer, you probably know what I'm talking about. Your brain wants to run free, and you have to be the bad guy who reins it in.

So let it play. Whenever you have a few unstructured moments—riding a bike, taking a walk, or even those moments when you have just woken up and are still comfortable in bed, let it work its magic and make connections in your stories that you couldn't see before.

I can't tell you how many "Aha!" moments have occurred when I let my writer brain off of its leash.

These moments often become the lifeblood of my story, moving the plot forward in really cool and unexpected ways that never would have happened without a little downtime.

Some of my author friends schedule their downtime between stories, taking a few weeks off to chill and play video games and let their minds really roam free.

Not me. I have too much to do, and too little time.

If you're like me, do what you can, and let your writer brain work its magic.

40 TIPS FOR NEW WRITERS

When you're just getting started as an indie writer, it can seem overwhelming. There are so many things to do and learn. If only there were a list…

And there is! Here are some tips I compiled from some of my author friends for you as a new author:

1) Start a Mailing List: But don't do what I did and wait for it to grow organically. Work on it. Promote it. Try joining some Prolific Works giveaways, or sites like Book Funnel or Story Origin to get new readers for your list. And take a clipboard to any convention or reading you attend, and be clear on what you need to do for any new mailing list sign up—get their express permission to be added to your list (a simple checkbox will do), and never force them to say yes for a free book or prize.

2) Making The Book is the Easy Part: We're writers. We know how to write. But when it comes to helping people to actually find and read the book, many of us feel hopelessly lost. Be prepared for a lot of promotional work once the book is in the pipeline and after it comes out, even if you are working with a publisher.

3) The Muddy Middle Slump is Normal: Slumps in the middle of the manuscript are normal, and the only way to get through them is to literally power through them. When I start to second-guess myself (and my sanity), I tell myself to write one more sentence, just one. Before I know it, I have another paragraph, then a page. After a couple days, that muddle in the middle starts to recede.

4) Promote a Little Every Day: Promoting is a lot easier when you do some each day. Set up a plan to do a few postings once a day to any social media sites you are on. Plan a regular blogging schedule, whether it's daily, weekly, etc. And reach out to other people in your own niche to share each other's books.

5) Keep a Strict Writing Schedule: Again, the secret is consistency. Have 15 minutes to write? Then try to write for 15 minutes *every day*. An hour? Even better. Tend to get lost in your writing? Your schedule will help you remember the important self-care stuff, like eating and sleeping.

6) Write What You Love: Don't try to write to the market. That way lies madness. You can try to catch trends, but usually you'll be the last one to the party. But if you write what you enjoy, that will show in your writing, and eventually it will bring you readers.

7) Be Wary of Long Multi-Book Contracts: One of my author friends wrote a short story for an anthology, and it ended up morphing into a series. She was scared that if a publisher didn't commit, she'd find herself in the position of publishing the first book and then not finding anyone willing to take on the rest. In the end, she was stuck with an eight-book contract, and was stuck writing stories in one universe for a very, very long time.

8) Tackle One Genre at a Time: Establish yourself in one genre before jumping on others—it helps your loyal readers to know what you write and makes it more likely that they will buy each new book you publish. I did not take this path, and have often regretted it.

9) Check the Publisher's Catalog Before Signing: Consider very carefully before contracting with a publisher that publishes few other books similar to yours. If they don't already sell your genre, how are they going to market and sell your book?

10) Don't "Write What You Know": It's not "write what you know." It's more like "learn about what you want to write, and respect the communities you write about." I'm a big proponent of writers writing whatever moves them, but I'm also a fan of respecting other cultures and people.

11) Everyone Hates Novellas: Everyone who reads your novella, even those who bought it knowing full well that it was a novella and not a novel, will criticize you for not making it longer. Take this as a compliment. They liked your writing and want more. And as my friend Stephen del Mar says: "Oh, they bitch if it's long too."

12) Do NOT Read Your Goodreads Reviews: Never, ever, ever read your Goodreads reviews. If you do, have a friend (preferably someone who knows what a wonderful writer you are) close at hand. Some writers ask that friend to glance over reviews, alert them to 4/5-star ones, and summarize the lower ones if there is anything useful.

13) Do Not Eat at Your Desk: If you do, you will not only gain weight but have crumbs in your keyboard, which can slow you down. When you're peckish, get up, walk around, take the dog for a walk, and grab a snack. Then come back to your clean keyboard and write some more. Note: I do make an exception to this rule for dark chocolate.

14) Wear Your Reading Glasses: If you use them, don't ever forget to wear your reading glasses while you're at the keyboard! You may think you can do without them, just that one time, and walk away with a headache that'll last days.

15) A Rejection is Just a Rejection: Rejection doesn't mean your writing sucks. It doesn't mean your book is bad. All it means is you haven't yet found the right home for your story.

16) You Are Your Idea's Slave: Once an idea has formed and needs to come out, you are its slave. Give in to it; otherwise it will never leave you in peace. I find this to be especially true at night when I'm trying to sleep. Many great ideas have been born at this time, and if I get up and write them down, they usually leave me alone for the rest of the night.

17) Read the Contract!: Always read your contract thoroughly, even if it's with a publisher you have already published with and it looks the same. One of my friends failed to spot a country jurisdiction change once, and now they read them thoroughly and check everything repeatedly before they sign.

18) You Need a Website and a Brand: Get a website, come up with an initial brand (logo, author photo, tagline), and get your stuff up there for people to find. Your own author website is the one place where you truly have control of your image. Keep it current.

19) Publish When You Are Ready: Don't let pressures from readers, finances, or your mother push you to upload until you are absolutely ready. Your book should be as perfect as you can make it (within reason) before you push that button.

20) Hire An Editor/Get Some Beta Readers: Your manuscript will have errors, ones you can't see because you are too close to it. Spend some money to get it edited, no matter how well-written your friends say it is. And similarly, a good beta (or three) can save you loads of aggravation down the road, helping you catch plot holes, sensitivity issues, and all kinds of other things you would likely miss by yourself, especially if your betas are well-versed in your story's topic or culture.

21) It's Mostly Luck: The business of publishing and selling your work is not a level playing field. Luck is a huge part of it. Below-average books can become bestsellers and excellent books can quickly disappear into obscurity. The cream does not necessarily rise to the top, and the feelings of resentment over that can eat you alive. The best antidote is to make connections, keep learning, and put out the best work you can.

22) Watch Your Bottom Line: Don't spend more money on a book than you will earn on it! It's really easy to do, with the costs of editing, cover art, proofing, and advertising all eating up your resources. Do what you can yourself (figure out what you are good at and learn as much as you can). Optimize your print book by tightening up chapters where they flow over to extra pages, remove blank pages, etc. to bring per copy costs down. And always be aware of what it's costing you.

23) Don't Work in a Vacuum: If you're having trouble getting accepted, even by small publishers, there are most likely *reasons*. Get help. Reach out to other authors and ask them to read your book. Don't think that you have to figure everything out on your own. There are so many other writers out there willing to lend you a hand. Search for a local writing group. Join online groups on your social media sites. Find your writing community.

24) Too Good to Be True?: If a publisher approaches you and gushes about your work and wants to sign you, and then has a contract that sounds better than anything else out there? Run. If it looks too good to be true, it probably is. Again, reach out to more experienced friends for a hand evaluating what they are offering.

25) Take a Break: Always give yourself some downtime. And make sure your breaks don't always involve more electronic screens. Get out into your garden, if you have one, or take a walk, or ride your bike to your favorite local coffee shop! Your eyes and mind will thank you.

26) Read it Out Loud: Read your writing out loud—it's a great way to catch errors your brain might miss otherwise, and to see where your phrasing is convoluted or confusing.

27) Never Respond to Reader Reviews: It will be incredibly tempting to respond to reviews, but for the sake of your sanity, *don't*. It's a rabbit hole you do not want to fall into, full of strange and dangerous things with teeth.

28) It's Like Homework—For the Rest of Your Life: As a professional author, you will feel like you have homework due all the time for the rest of your life. You'll never be entirely satisfied with your work. You'll simultaneously want to quit writing and feel like you're utterly incapable of quitting. But you probably already knew that.

29) Ignore Your Inner Critic: Don't let your own self-doubt keep you from promoting your work. We all have one. There's a name for this—it's called Imposter Syndrome, and every writer worth their salt has gone through it. Don't let it stop you from writing—instead, let it keep you humble, always ready to learn more about your craft.

30) Finish What You Start: Learn discipline and time management—*and* finish what you start! Many writers give up when the going gets hard. But if you want it badly enough, stick with the work until the bitter end.

31) Make Friends in Your Genre: Become friends with other authors who write in the same genre and cross-promote each other's work. These folks are great for commiseration, fleshing out ideas, and getting the word out about your latest book.

32) You're Probably in "Writer's Wait" for a Reason: When the words won't flow, it might be that your subconscious is trying to tell you there's one more thing you need to figure out about your story before you can write it all down. It's not a horrible thing if you take a little longer to think about a book before you write it.

33) Enjoy the Ride: Being a writer is a job like no other. We open our laptops or pull out our notebooks and dive headfirst into worlds no one else even knows exist. Celebrate it. Revel in it. And savor every compliment and good review you get.

Seven more quick tips:

- Deadlines can suck the fun out of writing.
- Edits and blurbs might make you scream.
- You won't become instantly rich.
- Promote your brand, not just new books.
- Make lots of friends on social media to help you.
- Do contests, try new things, and innovate.
- Above all else, support other authors and your community.

Thanks to the following authors for their submissions for this chapter: Amelia Faulkner, Stephen del Mar, Tabitha Creech, Wendy Rathbone, Rory ni Coileain, Heather Rose Jones, Christine Wright, Tali Spencer, LM Brown, Tory Phoenix, Alma Pagan, Bey Deckard, Angel Martinez, EJ Runyon, CB Lewis, Davina Jamison, Jeff Baker, Sorcha Black, and Aidee Ladnier.

UPPING THE ODDS

Some writers seem to have an innate sense of the publishing marketplace, surfing adroitly from one trend to another, catching every wave and riding it to success.

The rest of us aren't so lucky.

I've been writing seriously for over a decade, and I can't lay claim to riding a single trend to the top. Trends are, by nature, short and ephemeral—so unless you can turn around a book in ninety days (and some writers *can and do*) they are notoriously hard to catch.

My first book took me five years to write (and rewrite).

I finished the first draft of my second book in thirty days (during National Novel Writing Month aka NaNoWriMo), but it still took six months to go through two more drafts and a beta read. Then the publisher added six more for edits, so it took a bit more than a year from conception to publication. And that's *lightning-fast* in the traditional publishing world.

If I had any psychic forecasting ability at all, I might be able to see what trends were coming down the pike in six months to a year. Unfortunately all the crystal balls I've found have been murky and unreliable.

What's a poor writer to do?

Start with writing what you *want* to write. Sure, you can try chasing market, and *maybe* even catch it once in a while. But do you really want to spend the rest of your life writing things you don't enjoy, just for the off chance that you might get lucky once? You might as well take a job in corporate America—you'll probably make a lot more money that way too.

There's a reason you became a writer—to tell the stories swirling inside your writer brain. I'm not happy unless I'm writing, and when I do so regularly, I feel better about myself and about life in general.

So just write, and don't apologize for writing what you want to write.

But don't fret—there are ways to improve the odds without selling out your soul. These are less focused on the specific genre and characters (though you *should* generally be aware of overall genre popularity) and more on the current styles of writing.

A few meta trends I've noticed over the last few years:

- Telling stories with a clear, strong character voice
- Using first-person (especially in short stories) to give your story a sense of immediacy
- Dropping dialog tags wherever possible (he said, they screamed) and using character actions instead to identity who is talking
- Writing diverse character stories, while avoiding appropriation (a fine line to walk)

These are just a few I've noticed in my own genres. Research is your friend here. Read other authors in your niche—especially the really current stuff—and see what the trends are for yours that can help your work seem more in line with what readers, publishers, agents, and editors are looking for, *without* changing what you write.

And remember—writing is a process. We're born with the innate need to share our stories, and then we spend a lifetime figuring out how.

And if you're lucky, you'll eventually find a loyal base of readers who like what you do and how you do it.

THE WOLF UNDER THE TABLE

Sometimes we writers get stuck in a boring backwater, with nothing exciting at hand to move the story along. That's when this little sleight of hand trick comes in handy.

Let's say your characters are on a quest for the fabled *Sword of Bighands*.

They're sitting around a thick iron-banded wooden table at the Borderlands Pub, a dark, seedy, local hangout where you can buy anything from drugs to human slaves. Or a really good guide to get you out of Bordertown and across the great Scorched Desert, to the fabled Treasure Lands on the other side of that hot, dry, shimmering expanse of red sand.

Your characters are talking about the long trek ahead, sharing war stories, and sipping on curiously ice-cold mead. And they're absolutely bored out of their gourds.

So what can you do to liven things up?

Put a wolf under the table.

What would happen when your new pet wolf appeared in the midst of those tangled legs and began to snarl and bite at all the soft body parts within its reach under that beer-soaked table? When someone lost a finger (or worse) and people started to react with screams, falling backward out of their chairs and maybe even fighting back against our poor displaced wolf while the rest of the Pub looks on in startled confusion?

When your plot slows to a crawl, one of the easiest ways to fix it is to throw in an unexpected element that turns everything on its head, and sends the story racing off in a new direction. Just think of the questions this plot bunny raises:

- Why is there a wolf under the table?
- Who put it there?
- Was it there the whole time, and only woke up and snarled when someone stepped on its tail?
- Is it a werewolf?
- Why am I just standing here while said wolf slaughters my fellow questers?

I had a rather boring scene in one of my novels with several of my characters sitting in carriages, en route from the city to a manor out in the countryside. It was raining, and one of the POV characters was staring out the window, brooding on his life and his fate.

For a paragraph or two, it was fine, but after four or five, even he began to roll his eyes at me.

I needed a wolf:

Aik grabbed hold of the handle above the door, peering out into the falling rain. "I don't think so. It's—"

The carriage lurched forward and then down, sending him flying into the front of the cabin.

Aik caught himself with his right hand, saving himself from a probable broken nose. There was a horrid grinding sound, and then everything came to a screeching halt with the carriage laying at an awkward angle.

Boom. Wolf added. Okay, so it's not a *literal* wolf. Instead it was an unexpected and sudden event. The carriage had broken a wheel, stranding Aik and his two companions and their driver in the middle of an old iron bridge. They did the sensible thing and started to replace the tire. But sometimes one wolf isn't enough:

> *A low rumble quickly grew into a crescendo, and the bridge began to sway crazily under Aik.*
>
> *"Quake! Hold on!"*
>
> *Malin dropped the wheel, and it bounced away, rolling down the shaking bridge. He reached for the carriage, but a jolt threw him back against the rail, where he collapsed to the ground.*

Wolf number two—an earthquake—is just as unexpected, and immediately complicates the issues caused by wolf number one.

Now our boring riding-in-the-carriage scene has been transformed into a thrilling run-for-your-life one as our characters scramble in a mad dash to get off the bridge before it collapses. And as a bonus, our poor friend Aik still has all his brooding worries going on in the background.

These events also set things up nicely for a reveal of the secret Aik has been hiding from his best friend, which itself sends the story careening off in a new direction.

Plot wolves can take many forms—physical events, surprise arrivals of other characters, secrets revealed, etc. For a master class in this technique, check out the most recent version of *Lost in Space*. This show regularly releases two or three plot wolves per an episode, creating chaos and plot movement (and making the phrase "Things are not looking good for our heroes" run through my head almost constantly).

You do have to be careful about overusing this device, though. Wolves are an endangered species, after all. Too many plot wolves, and your readers may start feeling like sheep being fleeced with the same trick, especially if your characters escape unscathed *every single time*.

Still, the "wolf under the table" is a surefire way to add a little life to a tired plot arc and get things moving again.

And if you need some additional inspiration, I may have a pack of wolves (at a decent discount) to sell you.

While I have modified it, I first ran across this concept in a session given by author Damon Suede.

KEEPING A SERIES BIBLE

Fiction authors have a lot of things to keep track of in their books —character descriptions, locations, plot details, and all the other things that go into building a detailed and believable backdrop.

It's complicated enough creating an entire world for a single story. But what about when you want to write a series?

When you're working on a single story, the details are still fresh in your mind, and it's easy enough to flip back and forth through the text (or to use search) to find what you need. But writing a series multiplies exponentially the details you have to keep track of.

That's where the series bible comes in. A series bible is, at its heart, a compilation of facts about your world and the stories you set in it. It helps you provide a smooth, consistent experience for the reader, avoiding jarring missteps that occur when you forget what one of your secondary characters is called, or that your main city is on the shores of the Scayah Sea, and not on a river 300 miles inland.

There are almost as many ways to create and maintain a series bible as there are writers, and the right way for you is whichever one you are most comfortable with.

What App Should You Use?

- Scrivener offers an immersive writing app that will keep track of the details for you, but has a lot of moving parts.
- Dabble is a similar app that's a little simpler than Scrivener.
- Campfire is another world-building/series bible app that helps you "overcome disorganization," according to their website.
- One Note is Microsoft's note-taking app that also allows you to add other media (pictures, videos, etc.). Similarly, some folks use Evernote.

You can also do this much more simply—many folks use Excel, Word, or Pages to track the details, and some writers prefer to go real *old-school*, using the PPP method—Paper, Pencil, and Post-Its.

The *how* is less important than the simple fact of *doing it*.

I use a combination of Word for the general details and Excel for things like timelines that I want to be able to work with and sort more easily.

What Belongs In Your Series Bible?

The longer you write in a given universe, be it sci-fi, fantasy, or a sweet magical contemporary, the more the details pile up. It's up to you what to include. Here's what I usually have in mine:

- **Character Details:** Name spelling, hair color, eye color, height, race, history, relationships, and personal tics.
- **Place Details:** Stores and restaurants, real and imagined. Neighborhoods. Moon bases or starships or enchanted cities. Any place where the action takes place, or that's referred to in the story.
- **Cultural Details:** What do your characters and the people around them do for fun? Use for money? How do they govern themselves?

- **Plot Details:** Who did what to or with whom. Events both large and small, before and during your actual story.
- **History:** Whatever you need to know about how your world was founded, or how things ended up where we find them when your story begins.
- **Religion (Or Lack of One):** What do your people believe in? Why do they fight their wars? Or are they an atheist society?
- **Glossary of Story-Specific Terms:** This is especially true in genre fiction, and may include details like the names of alien creatures and plants, magic spells, etc. I often break these out into Food/Plants, Animals, People, Places, etc.
- **Story Slang:** Many stories have their own vernacular—idioms, ways of talking, etc., that may also vary from character to character. I create these on the fly, and then keep a list of them I can refer back to and re-use as the series goes on.
- **Timeline:** This is especially important when you have different characters who go off on quests in various directions, but ultimately need to end up back in the same place at the same time.
- **Ongoing Questions:** Why does my character bite his lip? Why do they wear robes on a hot world? Who started the whole "Frontier Pride Day" thing, and are they still alive? Note these as they come to you for quick reference and resolution later.

You may come up with additional categories, depending on your story and genre.

When Should You Start Your Series Bible?

This really depends on you. I open a new file for mine at the same time I start telling my story. For me it's something that grows organically, bit by bit, as I add details like bricks to the foundation of my story.

Some writers create much of their bible before they put the first word down on the page. This is especially true for stories that require a ton of research—historical or contemporary tales that rely heavily on a concrete sense of realism based on the actual world.

And for some authors, it happens once the story is written, in the editing phase, especially if they don't want to slow down their actual writing with constant trips over to the story bible file.

There's no right or wrong way here—try a few and find which one works best for you.

Okay, I Think I Got it. What Now?

Ready to dive in? Give these things one last think:

- How good are you at remembering minute details?
- What pieces of information will you likely need again for a later scene or story?
- What's the best way to organize the information / what works best for me?

It can be daunting, but the good news is that you don't have to sit down and write all of this out at the get-go if you don't want to. Sketch out the most important details at the start.

What color is the sky? Where is it set, and what are a few of the most important sense details of the place? Who are your main characters, and what motivates them? And what's your basic plot?

You can fill in the rest as you go.

When you're on book 14 in your series and you need to figure out when Frank met Xlindx or what color Hovith's *gerth* is, you'll thank your earlier self!

And don't be afraid to keep a little mystery in your series bible. As my friend Kari Trenten reminded me:

It's important for it to be contradictory and to contain information that can be interpreted in different ways with enough passion and zeal to create conflict in the universe for different characters who may well have a valid perspective or use it to justify the most outrageous behavior.

Thanks, Kari. Now, when someone points out an inconsistency in one of your series books, you can say with a straight face:

I meant to do that.

A FULL-TIME WRITER WITH PART-TIME TIME

I f you're a full-time writer, you may have so much time on your hands that you have a hard time finding enough stories to write to fill it.

I do *not* have that problem.

Stories swirl around in my head on spin cycle. They leak out in conversations, get themselves written down on napkins and bits of paper and note files on my Mac and iPhone and iPad. I have so many stories to tell, and so little time to tell them. You see, I'm a full-time writer with part-time time.

Now I'm not complaining, exactly. I have a wonderful husband, and we run a business together that keeps us fed, clothed, and reasonably entertained. But it would be nice to have a little more writing time. When you work full-time or more (I probably work 80 hours a week), it can be a challenge to find time to sit down at the keyboard to write, and to do so at a time when your brain is ready and engaged for writing. So you have to make the most of the time you have.

Consider Leaving Writing Altogether: This is a totally viable option. When you are feeling like you just can't handle it anymore, pull the plug. Shut down your blog, remove your Facebook author page, dump your assorted boxes of swag in the trash, and let your Publisher know you are done. Right, and after that, why not try swearing off chocolate for the rest of your life? You are addicted to writing, and you've got it bad. Why else would you continue to toil away at a job like this for next to nothing in pay and such horrendous hours? Face it, you're stuck with this lousy, wonderful job. So, with that out of the way...

Keep Good Notes: This one is very important, because after a while, the story you're writing about the winged man starts to shade into the one you're working on about the gay chef in Sacramento, and the short you promised to your podcast friend about the twelve days of Christmas. Before you know it, you look up from your writing daze and you've written a mangled scene about an angel mixing up a batch of brownies while humming "The Little Drummer Boy" under his breath.

Hydrate Regularly: This is always a good idea when you are writing, but especially when you are on a marathon run, trying to keep track of three different story threads. I recommend a case of Wild Cherry Pepsi. But if your characters are really giving you shit and your plot lines have hit a brick wall, you may need to hit the hard stuff—a trenta java chip peppermint mocha Frappuccino with extra whipped cream and chocolate syrup. You can practically feel your brain cells melting. Just warn your significant other ahead of time—they may want to clear out of the house for a few days. Or a week.

Eat Brain Food: All my normal joking about Oreos and Wild Cherry Pepsi aside, when you are getting ready to start an intensive writing session, eat a handful of nuts or something else with good protein to sustain you during the slog. Sugar will only take you so far, and you will crash hard. Think of writing as a marathon—your brain needs good food too to make it the distance. Besides, you can have the Oreos later as your reward for a job well done.

Schedule, Schedule, Schedule: And by this, I don't mean scheduling your writing. You're a writer. You write. And whether you can't help but write or just do it for the intrinsic joy it brings you, it's more important to schedule your eating and sleeping time. You know yourself—you've pulled all night writing binges and gone for days without a bite of solid food before, just to finish a story. But writing isn't a sprint, it's a marathon.

Pick a Writing Time: Set aside a regular time to write, and stick to it. This is one of the best strategies I have found for getting things done, as it forces me to focus on my writing. The tricky part? Avoiding the laundry's siren call two minutes before your writing time starts. Tell the laundry to screw off. It can wait.

Minimize Distractions: If you are working on a laptop or tablet, close EVERYTHING ELSE before you start. No Facebook, no emails, nothing. I use a great little app called Isolator that blacks out the screen and all other apps besides the one I'm in. "But I need my browser open for research!" you wail. Not a problem. You can open it when you actually need to look something up, and then close it again. Remember, your "writer brain" is like a magpie, always looking for the next shiny thing to distract it. Get a birdcage.

Buy One of Those Foot Massager Things: Face it, you're stuck at your little writing desk until the day you die, so you might as well enjoy your time there. I also recommend buying a scented candle (sandalwood is my favorite), a Snuggie, and some of those noise cancelling headphones. Hey, if you're never going to see the sun again, you may as well make your little writer cave comfy, right?

Don't Kill Yourself: Life happens. Sometimes your honey will drag you away for a surprise dinner. Or your Great Aunt Josephina will pass away unexpectedly, necessitating a last-minute trip to Kalamazoo. Or you'll sleep horribly the night before and your writer brain just won't engage. It's okay. It happens to us all. Take the loss, and re-engage tomorrow.

I hope these tips help some of my overwhelmed writer friends out there. Just one more—learn to say "No!" when someone asks you if you want to take on another project. I still haven't figured out how to do that.

SPICE UP YOUR STORY WITH SLANG

Looking for a way to spice up your somewhat flat and beige story? One way to do it is to pepper it with appropriate slang to give it some special flavor.

Whether you're writing a future world or something in the next city over, including local idioms and slang can add additional layers to your storytelling.

I once wrote a slow burn romance set in Antarctica. While I was writing it, I found a great site that includes some really cool Antarctic slang.

Here are a few, direct from Paul Ward at the CoolAntarctica.com site (with permission):

Antarctic 10: A person who might be considered a "5" on the attractive scale elsewhere.

Bolo: Burnt-out-left-over: an expeditionary who has been in the Antarctic for far too long.

Bunny Boots: Boots for extremely cold weather, large, white, and plain, but effective, the name comes from a layer of rabbit fur that's supposed to be part of the insulation (actually wool felt).

Country Mice: Scientists and their assistants who get to travel to camps around Antarctica.

Fingy: The pronunciation of **F.N.G.**. A derogatory term of uncertain origin for the F@!# New Guy (or Girl). Originally used in Vietnam to describe a solider on their first tour of duty.

Hollywood Shower: A naval term, derisively used to describe showers of longer than the allotted two minutes (fresh water in liquid form is relatively rare in Antarctica).

Manhaul: A sledging trip where the sledge is pulled by men rather than vehicles.

Nutty: The general term for any type of chocolate or sweets / candy, whether it contains nuts or not. A personal note here, when I first arrived in Antarctica, I was most unimpressed with the unhealthiness of the food that people took out with them when leaving base for a day trip—one to three bars of chocolate and nothing else. Being of sterner stuff I promptly made myself some healthy sandwiches (tuna and mayonnaise if I remember rightly)—I was observed with interest but without comment by other (wiser) people around. Come lunch break, while others tucked into their hard but edible "nutty," I sat and sucked on a frozen sandwich.

There are many more of these on the website, but you can see how much flavor they can add to the story.

Plus some of them are just really fun to say. *Jon went to get his bunny boots and grabbed a nutty for lunch.*

Of course, like anything else, you can go overboard, so be careful in your use of words that may be unknown to the reader, and sprinkle them in lightly.

A little *nutty* can go a long way.

TECHNOBABBLE

nother way to use vocabulary to spice up a story, especially a sci-fi one, is to include a bit of *technobabble*.

The Oxford English Dictionary defines technobabble as "incomprehensible technical jargon." Basically, in sci-fi, it's when a writer throws in a bunch of high-tech words to make their story sound all science-y:

Jelyk pulled the thromb-whistle to spin the arkensphere up to speed. Somewhere in the guts of the Hawkthorne, the mighty raction engines powered up, ready to thrust the massive ship into hyperspace.

See? I really know my technobabble. I bet you don't even know what an arkensphere is, but now you're dying to, right?

When done right, technobabble can add spice to your story, along with a sci-fi gloss that readers crave. But it can also go horribly wrong.

In my example above, I used three examples of the technique: *thromb-whistle, arkensphere,* and *raction engines*. I would probably have been better off with just one. If we already have a word for it, use that. A switch is a switch—why confuse the reader with something that makes no sense in context? And an engine is an engine.

But an arkensphere?

Oooh, I'll bet it's round and silver, but silver like mercury that ripples when activated, giving off purple bolts of static electricity, and it makes this really cool humming sound you can feel in your bones throughout the ship.

Now that's pure technobabble coolness.

In a similar vein, my sci-fi fantasy worlds often include a lot of made-up names for plants, animals, food, and other worldly and cultural details.

The general rule of thumb here is the same. If it's a horse, call it a horse. If it's truly something different—like three-legged drafting beasts or headless birds, then use a different word for it.

Once again, the key here is to not overwhelm the reader with weird, unknown words. Add them in slowly over the course of the story, explain them, and re-use them to reinforce their meanings over time.

Descriptive words are great too—when you think of a *flop tree*, you'll probably picture a tree with oversized, floppy leaves, right? Which is exactly what I intended.

Finally, make your made-up words pronounceable wherever possible. Too many *zylchs*, *mflligms* and *jxllntys* and you'll lose your reader.

So throw technobabble and alien words into your own work. They have the power to add a gloss of mystery and epic speculative fiction coolness to your story. Just be aware of *how much* and *why* you are using them, and don't go overboard.

And then beta reader the heck out of it.

WHEN THE WORD IS THE STORY

Sometimes it's hard to find the inspiration for a new story. Especially a short story. But I have a little trick to share with you.

I've always had a fascination with words. Makes sense, right? It's one of the prerequisites for being a writer, just like a love of the law is for being a lawyer, and a love of art is for the artist.

But recently, I've found a new, more specific use for this logophile obsession of mine—turning a single word into a story.

One of the questions many of my writer friends hate the most is "where do you get your ideas?" My friend Angel's flippant response is that she buys them wholesale at an idea emporium.

Their disdain is understandable—many writers swim every day in a sea of ideas, and pinning down one supposed source is all but impossible, so asking this is like asking us, "So how do you breathe?"

Still, there *are* some interesting places, things and ideas we writers occasionally turn to for inspiration, and words themselves are one of them.

One such idea is to start keeping a list of words you run across that you find interesting, especially words that were unfamiliar to you.

A couple years back, when I was working on the first book in the

Liminal Sky series, one of our pastors was talking about John the Baptist, and how he lived on the *liminal* edge of society at the time.

My writer ears perked up. What was this new word… *liminal*?

So of course I looked it up:

lim·i·nal

/ˈlimənl/

1. of, relating to, or situated at a sensory threshold
2. of, relating to, or being an intermediate state, phase or condition*

Given that the Liminal Sky series is about the transition of humanity from a planet-bound to spacefaring race, the word seemed amazingly appropriate for the work, and I adopted it as my own. It became not only the series title, but the word used to describe kids born with enhanced abilities in the series, and changed the course of the work.

But I'll give you a couple more recent, even more direct examples of how a word can become a story.

Another churchy word—*eventide*—came up in a hymn one week, and again got my attention. I love this word… it's basically just a synonym for "evening," but it's so weighted with antiquity and poetic beauty.

e·ven·tide

/ˈēvənˌtīd/

1. the time of evening

The word inspired a short story of mine of the same name, about the end of the universe a la Douglas Adams' "Milliways"—the restaurant at the end of the universe.

And while I was reading an Italian language novel called *Quando Tutto Inizia* (When Everything Begins) by Fabio Volo, I ran across the word *pareidolia*—it's the same in English and Italian:

par·ei·do·lia

/ ˌper.aɪˈdoʊl.jə /

1. The tendency to perceive a specific, often meaningful image in a ransom or ambiguous visual pattern*

Basically, it's when your brain sees something in a random pattern that isn't actually there. Like when you look up and see a castle in the clouds in the sky. Or that chicken leg I stared at for years in the stucco in front of the toilet in my mom's front bathroom.

And *bam*, my mind was off in another direction with a story of a boy who not only *sees* things in random patterns but then actualizes them.

There are so many words out there in the English language—171K by one recent estimate—that the possibilities for a writer are nearly endless.

The dictionary is your playground, but some of the best candidates come from folks around you and your everyday life. So collect words that interest you, and when you need a little inspiration, dip into your list.

You never know what they might inspire.

Thanks to Merriam-Webster for the definitions.

HIDING EASTER EGGS

When you are working on a story that's related to another one you've already written, a great way to reward your regular readers is to put little things into the writing that only they will recognize.

As an author, one of our main jobs is the art of making connections. Connections between characters. Connections between the beginning and end of a story. Connections within a series.

As part of this job, I often re-read older books in the same series as I prepare to write the next one, so I can make connections between the books that will give my readers that "aha!" moment when they discover them, and that will help ensure continuity between the stories.

But there are other kinds of connections that we use as writers, too.

Some are unintentional. These often come out of our subconscious writer mind, or sometimes from nowhere at all. These are of the "same character name in two stories" variety, or perhaps a location shared by unrelated stories that use it in different ways.

For instance, two of my stories have characters named Jameson, though they are very different characters separated by a vast gulf of space and time.

And keen readers will notice a certain nurse in Tucson pops up in two different books set in two different universes.

Okay, so that one *was* kind of intentional. It falls more under the "Easter Egg" category, and is fun for my readers to find.

The term Easter Egg (when used for hidden content) came originally from the video game world, where designers would often add secret bits that you could only access by typing in a certain code or knowing where to click or how to perform a certain action.

There were whole books devoted to sharing them, and there was always a little thrill when you discovered one on your own.

As a reader, I love these, and as an author, it's fun to plant them and see if anyone recognizes them when they read your stories, and sometimes they find ones even you didn't know you'd put there.

That's one of the reasons why writing fiction is such a magical art.

SUCK A LITTLE HAPPY JUICE!

A writer's life is a hard road. We try to stay strong in the face of rejection. We try to project optimism into the world, because that's what we want to come back to us.

But damn, sometimes it feels impossible.

I struggle with my inner critic, that voice inside my head that tells me I have no business being a professional writer. That I'm not good enough. That I *suck*.

But rather than wallow in all the messages it's giving me, I thought it would be better to share the ways in which I deal with it when I'm feeling like the fake-est, phoniest, most loser-y writer who ever lived.

So here are my strategies for coping with imposter syndrome. I hope they're helpful to you, too:

Reread Some of Your Good (Professional) Reviews: One easy way to counteract the self-loathing you're feeling is to remember that lots of people believe in you. Go back and look at some of your great reviews from the past, from professional reviewers or some of your regular readers, and remind yourself that your writing isn't nearly as awful as your IC would have you believe. Believe your fans.

Undermine the Bad: Go hard at whatever set you off (metaphorically, of course. Don't show up on some poor editor's doorstep). Round up your writer support group (i.e. your writer besties) and tell them what happened. When I get a bad rejection, mine remind me that a) everyone, even agents and editors, has different tastes, b) sometimes they just have a bad day or are busy and aren't in the space to connect with a story, and finally c) that even what sounds like a specific critique of the work may in fact just be their standard rejection form letter. Back away slowly, connect with your friends, and don't take it personally.

Do Something Good for Yourself: Clean yourself up. Dress up a little, even if you're not going out anywhere. Treat yourself to an extra-long, hot shower or bath, a nice cuppa whatever makes you happy, and try to remember what life outside of the writer cave looks like. Try to feel a little more human and a little less like a failure. Feel better by looking better.

Make/Review Your Accomplishments List: Write down all the things you have done during your writing career that you never thought you would accomplish.

- Published your first story? Check.
- Your first novel? Check.
- Made your first $100? Check.

When imposter syndrome gets you down, look at this list. And remind yourself how impossible each of those things seemed at the time. Every big step seems impossible—until you accomplish it.

Stick to the Plan: Do you have a plan for your writing career? Imposter syndrome makes us question our judgment and our plans. But as my friend Erik reminded me, you have to give these things time to work. No matter what your path, success doesn't usually come overnight. So take a deep breath, keep calm, and carry on. Hey, if it's good enough for the Brits, it's good enough for us, right? There will be time enough later to change course, if need be. But you chose this one for a reason, and you need to let it play out.

Do you feel like a legitimate author now that you've run through these steps? Probably not. Imposter Syndrome is real, and it eats at you bit by bit, seizing on each of your "failures" and supposed shortcomings to build a narrative designed to convince you that you really suck at this whole writer thing. It's not something you can magically snap yourself out of.

But you *can* start building yourself a new narrative—a story about yourself where you may be walking through the darkness now, but somehow you will always manage to find the light.

The story where you do *eventually* get where you're going, every time, if you just work hard enough at it.

And the one where you are good enough to do this whole *writing thing*, and you know you are because so many people have told you so.

As writers, we may receive ten fantastic, glowing reviews of our work, and then one bad one shoots all the rest down. We're so ready to believe the worst about ourselves and so slow to believe the best.

I've had some great moments as a writer—when I sold my first book. When I sold my second one and proved it wasn't just a fluke. When I got a fantastic review. When I made a reader ecstatically happy with one of my stories.

You have those moments too, if you just let yourself remember them.

We need to bottle up all those great things and put them away, ready to be opened at a later date when things don't seem quite so rosy. When imposter syndrome runs us down, it's time to grab that "bottle" of "all the great things," off the shelf.

Got a rejection? Open that file and relive some of those wonderful things folks said about you and your writing.

Latest book sales in the gutter? Take a ride on the happy memory train.

Hit with a horrendous edit? Suck a little happy juice.

With life and the world in such a weird, precarious, and sometimes downright awful place, you have to grab the good when you have it.

There's a reason I chose the name of this chapter as the title of this book. I wanted to remind you what a unique and glorious thing this author gig is. I want us to feel joy when we think about writing, and to carry that with us to our readers.

So hold those precious moments close, and when you need them, suck a little happy juice!

PART FIVE
READY, EDIT, GO!

Now that you've gotten your story out onto paper (or at least into a digital form in the bits of ones and zeroes in your computer), what comes next? Edits! Lucky you.

A LITTLE PHILOSOPHY: GARDENING IS WRITING

Recently, I ran across a framed image at a Starbucks, of all places, that reminded me of the art I used to draw when I was in high school. I sent it to one of my high school art teachers who I'm friends with on Facebook. She still has a bit of my art after all these years.

She acknowledged how similar it was, and then mentioned how focused I would get when I was creating art—that I would just block out all the raucous noise around me and become invested in the work. She also suggested that I should start to draw and paint again.

I thought about it for a while, and then it hit me—I do much the same when I go out into the garden each day to water the plants.

It's a sanctuary for me, a place to feel the sun on my face, the breeze on my arms. Where I care for the plants in their neat little pots and see how all the little steps I took over the last five months helped create such a beautiful, serene place. That's also how I feel when I get deep down into the roots of writing.

But the parallels between the two run far deeper.

As writers and gardeners, we carefully select the seeds or young shoots from which to grow our garden. We nurture them, taking care to pay attention to each separate plant, just as in writing we manage our individual plot and character arcs. We prune them back where needed, stripping out the extra growth that weakens the whole.

Sometimes we run into danger—like the spider mites that have decimated my tomato crop year after year. We reach out to others with gardens of their own to learn how to overcome these challenges, like spraying on a bit of organic neem seed oil to keep the mites at bay. Or when we write, trimming out the part that never fit quite right.

Sometimes our work is exclusively for our own enjoyment, and sometimes there's enough bounty to go around. And as the season draws to a close, so does our work, as we wind it down to its conclusion and ready ourselves for another round. Another garden. Another novel.

This year's green novel is filled to overflowing with tomatoes, peppers, and basil that needs a good trim, lest it come to flower too soon. Still problematic are the zucchinis that die on the vine more often than they ripen to maturity, like plot ideas that never quite pan out.

Every year, every garden, every novel, you get a little better at this, learn a bit more, create a more beautiful thing.

And it's in the fallow season, that dark wintertime when the plants are gone, the temperature drops, and the old vegetable flesh decomposes slowly into the soil, when our ideas for a new garden are born.

Then once again we sink our hands into the soil, enriched with the knowledge of seasons past, and coax from it the green shoots that will form a new masterpiece.

Every year, we get a little better at creating something wild and new.

THE FIXIT LIST

The manuscript is written, it's gone through your beta readers and is finalized in third-draft. Soon it will be ready to go out to the publisher/agent/pitch wars/wherever you plan to send it.

Almost.

There's still one last step you should take before unleashing your work onto an eager and unsuspecting world. Side note: can someone be both eager *and* unsuspecting?

It's time for the fixit list.

Every author who has been around for long enough has one. It's the list of things you know you do wrong, the ones you've been called on again and again by your editors but somehow never stop doing in the heat of writing.

I keep mine in Excel, but you can use Word, a journal, or even the coaster from the bar where you drank away your writing sorrows last night. Just start one, and add to it every time you become aware of another thing you do regularly in your writing that you want to curb.

Once you have your list, pull it out and methodically start working your way through the manuscript one last time, fixing all of those little things. And while it won't ensure a perfect manuscript (if you ever figure that secret out, *please* let me know), it can help you turn in a much cleaner one, and start focusing on not making those errors in the first place.

Here are my main fixit things:

But…: I'm a big fan of starting off sentences with conjunctions for effect. And it can work really well, giving your sentences a different meter and making your reader pause for a second. But used too much, it can become obvious and tiresome. And you never want your writing to be tiresome. And so, put your conjunctions where they belong, for the most part, and only start off with them when you really have to.

Then—he paused…: I am also crazy for em-dashes and ellipsis… again it's all about creating the pause—where you most want it—and varying your sentence meter… so your rhythm doesn't become—let's be honest —boring. But again, moderation is a virtue… so I usually cut out half of these in final edit. And remember… is for trailing off mid-sentence, while…. is for the end of a sentence.

He felt distant: I'm also really bad about using perception words as filters. You understand that I am telling you this, and you can feel that it's true. You may have heard that filtering actions through perception filter words—appeared, felt, saw, knew, realized, watched, etc.— distances the reader from the immediacy of the action. Now you can understand how it can bog down your writing. Dump these wherever possible—and don't *feel* bad about it.

It's a little annoying: I also like to use size modifiers as shades of gray, even though it can be a bit bothersome to the reader, if not also a little distancing too. Why say she was a bit tired, when you can just go with full-on tired? Yeah, I know, that's a little misleading. Sometimes you really *do* want that shading. But look at how often you do it, and again remove it except for the places you really want to use it to a little effect. You'll get more punch for it, if you do. At least, a bit.

That's beginning to bug me: My characters are forever beginning and starting things (and rarely ending them, damn them). Beginning with your next book, try dropping most of these. Start using them less, and soon you will only be beginning things when they really need most to be begun.

It's far *form* over…: We all have a dreaded word or two that we can't, for the life of us, ever spell right the first time around. Mine is "from." I can't tell you how many times my characters have run *form* danger, or taken the magic ring *form* someone else. So with every manuscript, I dutifully search for all the "forms" and change the ones that are wrong back to "from."

He said (and grunted and shouted): "I don't use dialogue tags (he said, she said) except when they are absolutely necessary to distinguish the speaker," he said. Then he shouted, "Instead, I use character actions, which also give me the opportunity to insert a little more color and description into the story." He elaborated, whispering: "So in the end, I search out all remaining instances of 'said' and replace them with character actions wherever possible."

They nodded, almost breaking their neck: One of the character actions I use is the nod. *nods* My characters are generally very agreeable sorts, and they are almost constantly nodding. Too much of this and it starts to stick out, especially when it's at the beginning of each paragraph. Find these repetitive gestures and prune them back like weeds.

I found myself passive: I'm also a massive over-user of the passive voice, managing to use it far too often in my work. Like perception filters, this can have the effect of causing your writing to seem distant, unapproachable. Much better to do something than to be *able to* do it, or to *find oneself* doing it. I do find value in using the passive tense—sometimes we really do want to remove the agency from our characters—but it can be easily overused. Just be aware of when and why you are using it.

I started this, finishing it: Ah, the Impossible Simultaneous Act (or ISA). I opened the door the other day, walking through it, and I got filled with splinters. ISAs are conjugated verbs followed by a verb infinitive, which suggests the secondary action is taking place at the same time as the first, being sometimes an impossibility. Search for these, and change the second verb to something like "and then he…"

Learn from your editors and beta readers each time they send you a list of recommendations. Watch for patterns in your writing, issues that draw attention to themselves when the reader should be paying attention to your story. Write them down, and the next time you're almost ready to submit, work through them and clean them up.

Your future editors will thank you.

WHY I LOVE SECOND DRAFTS

The second draft is one of my favorite parts of writing.

Why, you ask?

Because you don't have to push your poor little writer's brain to be extra creative and come up with all sorts of new things, like you do in first draft.

The story is still fresh to you—in fact, it's the first time you actually get to take a step back and view it in its entirety. It's like a mural that has to be painted section by section, but then appears in all of its (hopefully) stunning glory when you can finally step back to see the whole thing.

The second draft is also a chance for you to take a deeper dive into the world you've created, using your writer's pencil to sketch in all the beautiful details. Where before the sky was a "scary blue dome", now it's "an overarching arc of blue dotted with fluffy white clouds, overwhelming in its openness to someone who had lived their entire lives underground."

And there are no external critics yet. No one else has seen it—just you. It hasn't gone through beta readers or editors or advance readers or reviewers. For just a little bit longer, I can imagine that it's perfect in every way.

Over the years I've developed my own method for writing and

redrafting a story, one that helps me make the most of the story while not wearing out the text through overly extensive rewrites.

I start with a first draft, which I very rarely change except to fix continuity issues as I go. I keep moving forward at a steady pace, and keep a list of any issues I become aware of along the way.

As I'm writing the first draft, I'm constantly making notes as I go about plot holes, thin descriptions, and characterization / motivation. Here are a few of them from my current project:

- Show more of the training field in use
- More about the hydro dam
- Create a card game with different suits that Raven is proficient at
- Add light/lamps to what's in the box
- Need better names for the clans, the desert dwellers, and the highlanders. Resolve steader/farmer highlanders from cheff/clan highlanders
- Flesh out the "gods" religion.

Some fixes are easier than others. In my second draft, I start with those, either making the minor changes right away or placing a note at the appropriate part of the manuscript to deal with it when I get there.

Using brackets [ ] to highlight my notes makes them easy to find later:

[need to flesh out the religion a bit here]

Once I finish the easy ones, I make an action list of issues that need a more in-depth reworking throughout the story. This may include strengthening or changing certain aspects of the characters, threading in certain plot elements, or fleshing out world-building elements. I try to keep this list down to a single page, and then bullet-point each item in large, bold type so I can quickly review it before each drafting session.

This is the heart of my second-draft work.

Finally, I get out my project tracking spreadsheet—it's basically an Excel file, with columns for:

- Chapter #

- Scene #
- Characters in the scene
- Day / date
- Short description of the scene action

This is hugely helpful in synching up the plot when your characters wander away from one another, and also super handy if you need to create a synopsis of the story later on. Just paste the scene description into a word file and clean it up.

Then I dive into the manuscript, smoothing out the language, adding world details, and working on all of the elements on my list.

It's a time-intensive process, but if you do it right, the story comes out a lot stronger at the end, just in time for your beta readers to rip it to shreds.

Cue pack of wild dogs howling here.

WHY YOU NEED SOME GOOD BETA READERS

Speaking of beta readers—if you don't know what a beta reader is, it's someone who reads an author's story and gives it a critical review before the author submits the book to the publisher, giving us the chance to fix any egregious errors or plot misfires before the editors see the story.

I love my beta readers. I hate my beta readers.

It's a private joke between me and a friend of mine that, just once, I want all of my beta readers to agree that my manuscript is perfect as-is. Spoiler alert: it never is.

As authors, we are too close to our own work. We can't see the problems with it, the nuances outsiders pick up on when they read it fresh. From finding simple grammar errors and misspellings to helping unwind the more complex stuff—when the plot goes awry or there are major consistency errors or pacing issues—beta readers are immensely valuable to any writer.

And yet... when you've been working on a story for months and months, and have a limited time before submission, and a beta reader points out something major you have to fix... like I said, I love them and I hate them. But I couldn't do this whole *writing thing* without them.

One of my books had gotten good reviews from most of my betas, but it took one person in particular to crystalize what was wrong with it. An important character got short shrift in the final part of the story. It was something that other betas sensed or touched on, but it took this particular beta reader to identify it and point the way to a solution.

The change made the book much stronger, but coming just ten days before my submission deadline, it caused me a whole lot of heartache and soul searching.

When working with a beta reader, the most important thing is to set expectations up front:

Tell Them Exactly What You Want: The first thing you need to do is to set the ground rules. Some authors want just a high-level storyline critique:

- Does the plot make sense?
- Do things move along well?
- Are there any continuity issues?

Others may want more:

- Is the grammar right?
- Are there any typos?
- Does the text itself flow well?

And it can vary from manuscript to manuscript—a third draft will (hopefully) need a lot less work than a first draft. So be clear about the scope of the beta read, and agree on this before you get started. Then you won't get a manuscript that's been cut to shreds, when you only wanted to know if the main character was likable.

Remind Them Not to Slice and Dice Your Text: If this is the first time someone has beta'd for you, they may be tempted to just go ahead and make changes to your document. Remind them to suggest, not change.

Be Clear About How Suggestions Should Be Relayed to You: Do you want them to use track changes in Word? Would you prefer that the document be edited in a group document in Google Docs? Do you want a line-by-line summary separate from the actual story? Be clear from the start how you want to receive their changes and suggestions.

Be Realistic About the Beta Readers' Time: It takes a while to beta a book, especially if you're after something deeper than an overall impression of the plot, world-building, and characters. So give your betas plenty of time and a clear deadline. How long is the story? How many words can they realistically read in a day? Set a finish date that won't kill them and annoy you when they don't meet it.

Keep A List of Your Good Betas (And the "Bad" Ones): No one sets out to be a bad beta, but sometimes a beta is just not compatible with a particular author. Either they don't get *what* the author writes, don't like the story matter, or they just critique in a way the author is uncomfortable with. If someone does a great job, by all means ask them again on the next story. If they don't work well with you, leave them off your list the next time, but thank them for their time and effort.

Remember, It's Your Story: This one is really important. Every time I critique or beta a story for someone, I include this statement:

"But remember—this is your story, and you know it best. Please use what makes sense, and throw away the rest."

Yeah, I know this sounds obvious, and as authors we all should already know it. But including those two little sentences gives the power back to the author, and indicates that you won't have a problem if they reject some (or all) of your suggestions. Remember, when someone betas for you, that it's *your* story, and you are free to embrace or reject any suggestions given.

Beta readers can be a huge boon for an author, helping you to identify and fix weaknesses in the story before it's submitted and/or goes to print. Cultivate your betas, and let them know how much they mean to you. Your writing (and your readers) will thank you.

SENSE & SENSITIVITY

As a writer, it's important to stretch yourself—to write about things (and people) who are unfamiliar to you.

It's one thing to create a race of aliens that has nothing to do with the human race—then you can pretty much go hog wild with however you want to portray them. Unless you unwittingly tap into some negative human stereotypes—Jar Jar Binks, I'm looking at you.

But what about when you're writing about an existing human culture?

I'm a gay man. I can write gay characters pretty much with impunity, because they're not just what I know, but what I am.

I'm also a white cisgender American, and feel pretty comfortable writing those kinds of characters.

But how about writing a woman? I've lived my entire life around them—mother, grandmother, aunts, cousins, friends, TV and film characters… while I am not a woman, I think I'm on fairly stable ground with female characters.

But what if I write about a lesbian? Sure, we have the same sex orientation thing in common, but there are a lot of differences, including how we experience the world.

Moving farther away from my own experience, what about someone who is bisexual? Who is Black? A Korean character, or someone who is transgender or gender fluid or non-binary?

As writers, we can imagine all of these things, and we're free to commit those imaginings to paper. It's kind of what we do.

But we also have to realize that these imaginings are ultimately based on real people and real cultures, and that when we write about them blindly, we do so at our peril.

This is where sensitivity readers come in. A sensitivity reader is typically someone who shares important characteristics with a character (or characters) in your story that you may not feel fully comfortable (or qualified) writing. In a nutshell, they are there to vet your story for any pitfalls that you can't see yourself.

I've used sensitivity readers a number of times, for trans characters, a deaf character, someone who was non-binary, and even a character with OCD. Each time they have helped me identify issues with my writing which would have been offensive to the community I was portraying, saving me heartache and grief and allowing my readers to enjoy the stories without having to deal with my ignorance.

But the hardest one was for a novella that was explicitly about race.

It was set on another planet, in another culture, so I thought I was home free in my portrayal of the Black characters in the story. But just to be safe, I asked a friend who is also an editor and a sensitivity reader to look it over for me.

When she said we needed to talk, my heart just about stopped.

We had a long, face-to-face discussion about the story, going from point to point. I won't bore you with the details. Essentially, my characters were acting in ways that just felt wrong to her, based on her own lived experience as a Black woman.

I tried the "but it's another world" defense, but she had a simple reply that made a lot of sense in retrospect. Yes, my story may be set on another world, but it's being read by people—including Black people—on our own world, shaded by all of their own experiences.

I sat back, took a deep breath, and got to work on what she'd said, and in the end, it's a much better (and much stronger) story for it.

Sensitivity readers are not about strangling your work. They're not about telling you what you can't do. They're more like lamp posts, illuminating a world we'd only seen dimly, and providing a clear path through for our stories.

If you were writing a story about race cars, you'd go to a race car expert to find out what you needed to know, right?

This is no different.

So write what you want. Really! Go out and explore the world and its cultures through your work.

But don't be afraid to ask for a few lanterns along the way.

THE PERFECT TITLE

S o you've finished your book, and it's time to change your *working title* into your *forever* one—the one that will stick with your newly finished work for the rest of its happy little book life.

So how do you choose the perfect title?

At their best, titles do a few key things for your book. They make a bold statement about what the reader will find inside. They convey (along with the font and cover art) the genre of your story. And they tease the reader and invite them inside.

A good title should be:

Relevant to the Story: I love it when someone reads one of my stories and tells me that the title just works—it evokes the storyline, sometimes even offering a little more insight. I always strive for my title to have a strong connection to the plot of the work.

Easy to Read/Understand: Titles (and sometimes their presentation on your cover) that cause confusion will turn your readers off, and can result in lower sales. For *Chinatown* (which totally violates the next rule, but it was just what I wanted for the story), the title was meant to confound expectations, and in this vein I ran it sideways along the left side of the cover from bottom to top. This, along with the retro sci-fi font I used, confused many folks and muddied my story message, so I reworked it until I had something that most of my test subjects (you probably call them friends) loved.

Unique in the Marketplace: This isn't always possible, but if you can, find a title that's not already used by a hundred other books. One of my first published novellas, *Between the Lines*, is almost impossible to find on Amazon because it's too common a title—on the first five pages alone, I found 52 books with the same title, making it a poor choice even if it perfectly suited the storyline.

So now that you know what a title should *do*, how do you choose the perfect one? Authors come up with book titles in many different ways. I've used a number of different methods myself:

The Inspiration Word: As I mentioned earlier, sometimes a word can inspire a story. *Pareidolia* and *Eventide* were both words that I ran across in the wild that inspired stories, and they also became the eventual titles.

A Song Title: "I Only Want to Be With You" got its title from the Vonda Shepard version (a la *Ally McBeal*) of the old Dusty Springfield hit, although the story itself was inspired by Vanessa William's "Save the Best for Last." *Wonderland*, my ironically titled post-zombie apocalypse Christmas tale, took its title from the song "Winter Wonderland." And *Flames* came from Bastille's song "Things We Lost in the Fire," which helped inspire the story.

Made-Up Words: Speculative fiction offers us the opportunity to make our own words, "borrowing" them from the worlds in our stories. *Ithani* and *Skythane* are both made-up names of races in the Oberon Cycle trilogy, and therefore unique on Amazon's bookstore (though it turns out that *Ithani* is *actually* a word in both the Kannada language in India, meaning "of whom," and in the Xhosa language in Africa, meaning "an answered prayer," which is kind of cool).

Pulled Out of Your Ass: Many of my titles fall under this one—sometimes the "right" title just presents itself to you, and you can't shake it, even if it doesn't fit all the rules above. *Chinatown, Between the Lines,* and *A New Year* all felt like the perfect titles for their respective stories, but did not pass the "unique" test. Still, I went with my gut, and I'm not sorry.

What's Hot: Check Amazon's subcategories for your genre and see what the top books are using for their titles. While you don't want to steal someone else's title, this can give you an idea for what title formats are trending and point you in the right direction.

A Title Contest: I did this with my *Antarctica gay-trans scientist climate change romance*—I put it out to my friends and fans, and offered an Amazon Gift Card for the winning title. My friend Caleb nailed it with *Slow Thaw,* a title I knew was perfect the moment I saw it, because it encapsulated both the relationship and the melting of the Antarctic ice.

Once you have your title, look it up on Amazon and see if it's unique or if there are a few other books with the same one (or even hundreds). It doesn't *have* to be unique, but if the competition is stiff, you might consider tweaking it.

Congratulations—you now have the perfect title for your book.

And hey, if you decide later that it just doesn't work, you can always rename it for the second edition.

SHOULD YOU BECOME AN INDIE AUTHOR?

"Self publishing" has been around for a long time. Before the days of the internet (yes, I *am* that old), it used to mean using a "vanity press"—derogatory slang for a company that would print the books for you, and then leave a pallet of them on your doorstep. After that, the rest was up to you.

Some of these companies would provide marketing and other services, often at an exorbitant cost, offering dubious value for the work. The enterprising self-published author would then schlep their book around to local bookstores, events, and anywhere else they might make a sale, trying to build a reputation as a *real author*.

There was a stigma to the term "self-published," because it often did mean lower quality books written by someone who couldn't get a "real publisher."

How things have changed.

The advent of Amazon and other online book-publishing platforms means that it's now possible to reach readers much more easily as an *indie author*—the term many of us now use that more accurately reflects what we do and removes some of that old stigma associated with the idea of "vanity" publishing.

There is still a lot of "lower quality" work out there, but some of it now comes from the big publishing houses themselves, while AI presents a new and as-yet uncertain challenge that's pouring its own share of low-quality sludge into the mix—even if it's not (yet) capable of writing a cohesive, well-composed. and layered novel-length story.

So, is being an indie author the right thing for you?

Now that you've finished your opus, you'll need to decide which way you'll go for your book's publication. I'll lay out the main options for you to consider, along with their plusses and minuses.

Try to Sign With One of the Big Houses: Once upon a time, this was every writer's dream. With a big publishing house comes a chance for instant name recognition, a decent paycheck (*if* you keep writing *and* they keep publishing you) and marketing support that no smaller publishers can match. There's also a certain *cachet* that comes with being able to say you are published by one of the Big Guys.

But getting in can be difficult. Although some of the larger publishers will (very) occasionally have open submission periods, most of what's submitted that way likely ends up in the slush pile—the vast, usually unread folder of unloved manuscripts every large publisher has. It's not impossible that your beloved story will be plucked out of the slush pile —it has happened before—but it's very unlikely.

A more plausible path to a big publisher's list runs through their gate-keepers, the literary agents. Good agents have the ears of editors at the various big publishers, and know what they like. They take manuscript submissions and comb through them for books they think are likely to sell. There are tons of agents out there, some better connected than others. Most will accept your query—just be careful to follow each one's guidelines to a "t." But they, too, are overwhelmed by submissions, and it can take months (or in some cases over a year) before they respond.

One thing to keep in mind with a bigger house—unless you have what they think is one of the hot new books of the year, their marketing support for yours is likely to be minimal, so you will be left to do a lot of it by yourself.

And if your first book doesn't perform well enough, they may not pick up your next one.

I had an interesting conversation with a top agent who was both kind and very frank with me. She confirmed that agents aren't looking for the next great mid-list author—one who will sell steadily and reliably but not spectacularly over a long period of time. They want the next Stephen King or Jonathan Frazen—guaranteed blockbuster generators who will pad the publisher's (and the agent's) bottom line.

Keep in mind, too, that mergers are not uncommon at the top of the publishing industry, and your books may suddenly be under contract with a new company, with unpredictable results.

None of this is meant to discourage you. If you have your heart set on one of the big New York publishers, take your shot. You never know— you might end up with your name in lights, booked on the talk-show circuit and on a ten city book tour for your masterpiece. Just go into it clear-eyed, and be ready to pivot if that door doesn't open for you. It's not you, it's just the way the system works.

Choose a Smaller Press: There are thousands and thousands of small presses out there, some of which publish hundreds of books a year, and some that do two or three. Many of these do not pay an advance, and if they do, it may be relatively small. My first one was $500, and you have to sell enough books to generate that amount in royalties before you are paid any more.

But small presses are often nimble and dynamic in ways that the biggest publishers can't be. They are more willing to take a chance on untried authors, and a good small press will have a strong editing program, a stable of graphic designers to create professional covers, and a marketing plan to help get your book into the right hands. Their budgets for this are often very limited, so they (and you) have to be creative about getting the word out about your new book.

Small presses can also be problematic—lacking the resources of a big house, they can be slow to move the process along at times while they wait for incoming cash to pay for them. In the best cases, they can be vibrant, welcoming communities. In the worst, they can be more like a dysfunctional family.

If you are considering submitting to a small press, it's vital that you do your homework before approaching them. Do they publish books like yours/in your particular genre and sub-genre? How many books are they putting out a year? Do they have a fairly consistent publishing schedule (one a month, one every three months, etc) or are there long gaps between releases? What do their own authors think of them? Do they seem stable?

Many authors I know have gone through a small press closure, a few done in an orderly manner, a few sudden and unexpected. Some of them have gone through it two or even three times, and it's one reason many authors have ultimately gone the indie route.

You may go through a few before you find one that fits you and your writing the best, but publishing with a small press can be a great way to get your book out there with less effort and expense on your part.

Taking the Leap - Becoming an Indie Author: This path is the scariest of all, but could also be the most rewarding.

Let's look at the downsides first.

You have to do everything, and/or pay someone to do it for you. And I do mean *everything*—editing, proofing, book formatting, cover design, uploading to vendors, marketing and promotion, and customer service. There's a steep learning curve, and I won't lie to you—it's *a lot* of work.

You're essentially creating your own publishing house from the ground up, and if something breaks, you get to fix it.

Now for the upsides.

You have *complete* control. Don't like the cover? Redesign it (or find a new cover designer).

Don't like the editorial suggestions on your manuscript? You can ignore them (though think long and hard about it first—after all, that's why you hired an editor, right?).

Want to release the book the day after it's finished? You can! You don't have to wait on a traditional publisher's in-house schedule.

You also need to be relentless about your bottom line. Indie publishing is a numbers game. Everything has a cost, and the more you can learn to do yourself, the less the process of creating your finished book will cost you (and the more you will earn after those expenses). Still, it's important to know what you can do well, and what would be better done by a paid professional.

Is the whole idea of being an indie author daunting? Yes! But it also comes with great rewards. It's hard to describe the feeling when your first book—the one you built yourself from the ground up—finally arrives on your doorstep.

There will be times when you are absolutely ready to quit. When you throw up your hands and mutter some imprecation to the writing gods and decide you are done—done!—with indie publishing. But there will also be sublime moments of great personal satisfaction, when a glowing review, a grateful reader, or a writer friend who is in awe of your prowess reminds you exactly why you do this crazy thing.

And remember, none of these paths is irrevocable. You can start out at a big press and move to a smaller one, or vice versa. You can indie publish one project and then place the next with a traditional publisher. Or you can jump into being an indie author with both feet after a decade of someone else doing the work, and take it on yourself.

I started at a small press, tried for an agent and a big house, and ended up as an indie author who occasionally goes hybrid. It works for me.

So pick the one that sounds best to you, and give it your all. Sooner or later, you'll find the path that works best for you too.

IF YOU SUBMIT

So you've figured out what you wanted to write. You've done the hard work of actually writing and editing your story, conquering writer's wait and the muddy middle. There are wolves under tables, easter eggs, HSMs, and world building that would make your twelfth grade English teacher proud.

And now, if you've decided to try for a publisher instead of publishing your masterpiece yourself, it's all over but the waiting.

Writing is all about waiting. Waiting for inspiration. Waiting for story issues to resolve themselves in your subconscious. Waiting for beta readers and editors to get the book back to you.

But the worst of all of these is the wait after submission, waiting to see if what you wrote was good enough to make the cut.

None of us likes to wait.

So what's a distressed writer to do while waiting for the editor to get back to you (and hopefully tell you how much they want to publish your work)?

Work on Another Project: Dive into something new. Your writer brain is full of ideas—why not indulge one of them? Write another novel. Craft a short story for an anthology or magazine you want to get in, or pull out an old project and dust it off. Every moment you spend working on something new is a moment that you're not worrying about your submission.

Think About Your Next Move: What will you do if your story is rejected? Do you want to self-publish it? Send it off somewhere else? What is your ultimate goal for this work? Create a plan so you're ready if the editor rejects it.

Research, Research, Research: Now that you know what you want to do with your story if it is rejected, channel that into action. Want to send it to another publisher? Research the market—who else takes this kind of work? Who else is accepting new authors? Want to snag an agent? Research the possibilities—who are the good ones, and what's the best way to approach them? Want to self-publish? Research the process—how do you format a manuscript? Where should you submit it?

Clean Up Your To-Do List: What writing-related things have you been putting off while writing your opus? Work on your website. Do some backlist promotion. Make some new networking contacts. Plot out your next novel. Take a few courses to improve your writing skills and polish your style. Make the waiting time work for you.

Find Some Support: Last but not least, writers are human. We can only put off worrying about what someone else thinks of our book baby for so long. Find a few folks whom you can talk to privately—folks who will let you cry on their shoulders until your book is accepted, and comfort you if it's not.

Keep your worried little writer brain busy, and the wait will go by faster. Or at least it will seem to.

PART SIX
GETTING IT OUT THERE

Now that your book is ready to go, what next? And once it's published, how do you bring attention to it?

A LITTLE PHILOSOPHY: BEING ON BRAND

Every now and then, an author should give some thought to their "brand"—the sum total of how they are perceived in the world as an author.

I had reason to do so recently because of a few unrelated events.

First off, in a con panel on "going mainstream," we discussed authors' social media presence, and how any agent worth their salt is going to comb through it before offering to work with you. It makes sense, right? How many times have we seen old posts come back to haunt people years later? Even when those posts might have been justifiably called "youthful indiscretions." On the internet, your past lives forever.

The second thing was watching a famous fantasy writer read a fantastic sci-fi short online, live from his home. It was fascinating—the story of an alien encounter as seen by a cabin boy. The story managed to include both a sly space opera reference, an actual opera, and Humphrey Bogart. The thing is, I never even *knew* this author wrote sci-fi. I have only ever read his fantasy books. So it seemed "off brand" to me, but nevertheless I was like, "Dude, you need to do more of *this*."

And the last thing was this, a snippet I found on an agent page while reading her wish list:

"Lastly, I enjoy working with authors who show social media savvy and who haven't alienated one half of the nation or the other with intolerance."

So yeah. I kind of get it? Corporations (and *all* the big publishers are corporations) are *risk averse*. They want authors who write beautiful things they can sell, and who only share pictures of puppies and flowers on social media, keeping their political opinions to themselves.

They make it quite clear. Stick to your brand, and keep your damned opinions to yourself.

And yet…

In so many ways, this is a seminal moment in the history of the planet (which needs a big overhaul in the way we live if it's going to have any future *human* history). This is the time when everyone needs to stand up and speak out against what's wrong in the world.

Anyone who knows me also knows that I have not been shy on this point.

I want to make this part very clear. I am talking about myself and the way I have decided to present myself in the world, both personally and professionally. Each author has to make this choice for themselves, based on their own lives, their friends and family, where they live, and their comfort level—I'm not going to criticize anyone who feels like they can't make the same kind of public statements that I do, or who chooses to separate their public author persona from their private one with a pen name.

Those are both valid choices—and in all honesty, I might have been better off using a pseudonym from the get-go for this very reason. But I chose to publish under my own name. My Grandpa John told me to always be proud of my family name, and I nodded and said, "Yes sir." Besides, there's no going back now.

You can probably tell I've given this a lot of thought. Yes, I have been outspoken—and will continue to be—on social media about my politics. And yes, that might hurt me with some agents or publishers.

But here's the thing. Being outspoken on behalf of Latino kids in cages, of Black lives and trans lives, against corruption and for the health of the planet *are* my brand, or at least a big part of it. I am an openly gay man who writes a very diverse cast of characters in my fiction, and who portrays and works for a more hopeful future.

Any agent or publisher who doesn't get that about me, who thinks those are issues that should be stripped out of my social media pages and hidden away from public view, is someone I don't want to work with.

History will judge whether I was right or wrong, but this is a hill I am willing to die on.

My public, activist persona is part of my brand, and I'm good with that.

I hope when you figure out your brand—whatever it is—you feel the same.

THE NETFLIX EFFECT

When Netflix first switched from being primarily a DVD delivery service to creating and streaming their own projects, one way they distinguished themselves from traditional television networks was by dropping an entire season at once, singlehandedly creating the bingeing phenomenon. Instead of having to wait a week between each episode, you could suddenly just watch the whole season back-to-back.

The Netflix effect has been in evidence now for a while in series fiction—the idea that the author should have the whole series ready to go when the first book launches, so they can release them quickly, one after another, to allow people to binge read the series and not have to wait too long for the next book.

As a writer, I *hate* this idea—though I accidentally ended up doing this with one of my series. Did it work? The jury is still out.

This strategy works for Netflix because they're a multi-billion-dollar company, and they can bring a stable of writers, actors, producers, gaffers, caterers, and the like to the party to crank out a season in a fairly short period of time. And if it fails? There's another one just around the corner.

Individual writers don't have those resources. We sit alone in front of our laptops, writing day in and day out, using any little scrap of time we can scrounge from the EDJ and our other daily responsibilities.

What if you spend two long years writing three books in a series, and then the first one flops?

And yet...

Once your book is out, you are locked into what you wrote in that book. That's generally okay—you're the one that wrote it, after all. But you can't go back and erase inconvenient bits that don't fit the direction you want to go in for book two (or three, or four). You don't have a blank slate to work with; instead you're looking at a gnarled piece of wood and trying to figure out how to add onto it to make a beautiful piece of sculpture.

In some ways, maybe it would be much easier if you wrote all three of those damned books at once.

A good series bible and a reasonable outline can go a long way toward helping you avoid future pitfalls if you release your series books as you go.

But dammit, that Netflix thing is starting to look pretty enticing, too.

NARROW OR WIDE?

How do you want to sell your books? If you go the indie author route, that's one of the first questions you'll have to answer once your book is ready to publish.

We use the words "narrow" or "wide" to differentiate between two vastly different strategies.

Selling *narrow* means utilizing only one vendor—typically Amazon —and essentially putting all of your eggs in one basket. It can have its own rewards—typically, if your book is in Amazon's Kindle Unlimited (their all-you-can-read plan), it will rank higher on the Amazon website, which can translate into more visibility and higher sales. But remember, you are also subjecting yourself to the whims of one vendor. And if they ever decide to shut your account down, you are entirely at their mercy.

If instead you decide to go *wide*, it means you'll be selling your books through multiple vendors, spreading out your risk and giving you the opportunity to reach non-Amazon readers.

I started out my indie author life "narrow"—tethered to Amazon's ecosystem. It seemed like a good idea at the time. I had writer friends who were all-in on the online retailer, with their books also in Kindle Unlimited. KU is Amazon's all-you-can-read service that gives readers the ability to pay one flat monthly price and read any books that are currently enrolled in the program.

Which sounds like a win-win, right? But there are a few important caveats.

First off, the amount you are paid per page read varies from month to month, as Amazon decides how much money to put into the monthly "pot," and it also depends on how many readers read how many pages during that month. Although the monthly allotments have increased over time, so have the pages read. That's typically meant a decline in what's paid to authors for each page read, meaning you'll make less when someone reads your book via KU today than you would have a couple of years ago.

From my limited experience with the program, a book has to be around a hundred-thousand words long to make the break-even point—where you earn about as much on a KU read as you would on an eBook sale. For anything shorter, you're earning less, so you have to make it up in sales volume.

And don't get me started on how Amazon counts "pages," or how many imaginative ways scammers have come up with to skim off part of the money pot for themselves with fake reads and knock-off stories.

Still, Amazon+KU has worked really well for many writers. And as I mentioned above, when you release a new title, you typically get a bump in Amazon's book rankings if your new book is in KU.

My first few Amazon-only releases typically shot up into the 7000ish rank (of all eBooks being sold on the platform at that time) for a day or two. Granted, these were usually short stories priced at 99¢, so I made 30 cents a sale, and on the best one of these I earned $130. But after a few releases, even that limited success dried up—like a drug that loses some of its effect with each use—and my later releases no longer soared up Amazon's charts.

And here's the other thing about KU. It's an exclusive program. So if you sell your books in the Kindle Unlimited store, you can't sell them through *any other vendor.* That was ultimately what made me decide to leave the program.

My books are still listed at Amazon, but they are out of KU, and the vendor is no longer my primary focus.

When I committed to going wide a while back, I started selling my eBooks through Barnes & Noble, Kobo, Apple, Google Play, Smashwords, Payhip, and a number of smaller vendors, as well as Ingram Spark for print (for bookstores and libraries).

Many authors establish direct accounts with Barnes & Noble, Kobo, and Google Play, and do the rest via a distribution site like Draft2Digital.com, a great service that you can also use for free to generate downloadable eBooks. They only charge you if there's an actual book sold via their distribution channels, at which time they take a flat percentage of the sale.

Having direct accounts with Barnes & Noble and Kobo gives you some additional benefits too, including access to the promo options for these two sites. Each offers monthly promotions that you can apply to join, many of them free.

But if you'd rather not deal with so many vendors, you can also run those two via your Draft2Digital account and keep things simple.

Kobo, incidentally, offers the same kind of all-you-can-read program as Amazon, but they don't force you to be exclusive to their site.

Being wide means just about anyone can get your books, even folks who don't want to deal with Amazon, and there are many of them. And while it can take a while to build up sales via these non-Amazon venues, it can be done, and spreads out your risk. You're no longer at the whim of a single vendor.

I was reminded of this by a recent visit and discussion with a local bookstore owner. Bookstores often dislike Amazon because of how the retail giant has cannibalized the market. And although Amazon is happy to sell to bookstores too, store buyers rarely purchase from the online retailer, because bookstores run on the ability to return books that don't sell, and Amazon's sales are non-returnable.

Bookstore owners often strongly believe that authors should be promoting their own local bookstores over online retailers, and de-emphasizing Amazon in their sales channels.

And there's a way to do that, at least for print books. A site called Bookshop.org works with local independent bookstore owners and funnels the money back to those stores when they sell a book. If you have decided to go wide, it's a great way to both increase your sales and give something back to your community.

In the end, it's up to you if you want to stay in the Amazon pool, or venture out into wider waters. Each has its trade-offs, but there's no reason why you can't start with one strategy, and then switch horses if you find it's not working for you.

For me, I came down on the side of more consumer choice and in support of my local stores.

Amazon, I may never be able to quit you, but you're not the only game in town.

SHAKING UP YOUR
MARKETING PLAN

On paper, you've been doing all the things authors are supposed to do to market themselves and their works online. You have your Facebook pages (personal *and* Author). You are active on social media and have a great network of author and reader friends. You talk about yourself more often than you post about your works, showing admirable writer modesty.

You have an Amazon Author page, a Goodreads Author page, and maybe even author accounts on BookBub, BookBrush, StoryOrigin, BookFunnel, Prolific Works, and half a dozen other publishing-related sites.

You have your own writerly blog/website, with regular, unique content. The site has a beautiful, prominently featured "buy my stuff" section, with author comments and nice links to everything.

You have done Facebook ads, Amazon ads, massive blog tours, big review tours, and online podcasts.

You have been to multiple cons.

And yet, you're not a massively successful author, sales-wise. Maybe not even really a moderately successful one.

Maybe you need to try something new.

One day, stuck in my own marketing doldrums, I decided to try something different. I dragged my husband Mark with me, and we took a tour of Sacramento's coffee shops on bikes.

It was a 12-mile round trip, hitting just about every coffee house in East Sacramento, Midtown, and Downtown. I took along a bunch of promo cards for my latest book and plastered them on bulletin boards and on tables all across town, and on the way, I did some live videos on Facebook to promote the "tour."

Friends followed our journey, commenting on the videos and posts, and I was able to interact with them as we went. It was a lot of fun and great exercise, and it gave me a list of places I can stop by regularly, whenever I am near one of them, to refresh my stack of promo materials.

Did it bring more eyeballs to the story? Hard to tell. And there were a few things I would have done differently in retrospect, including more promotional lead-up time before the tour, and maybe reaching out to some of these places to involve them in it directly. And yet, it was amazing to get out there and do something physical to promote my own work directly to the public.

On another occasion, we did something similar with the Little Libraries in our area.

If you aren't familiar with these, a Little Library is a small bookstand (they look like oversized birdhouses on poles, and come in a wide variety of designs) where people in the neighborhood take and leave books for others to read.

Mark and I took a bunch of first edition copies of one of my books and did a tour of our neighborhood, depositing signed copies in each of about ten Little Libraries. Once again I documented the whole thing on Facebook, and (hopefully) made a few new fans.

The key thing here is to think outside of the box, and to take your marketing local as a way to find new fans.

A few other marketing and promo ideas:

Do A Blog Tour: This is a mainstay of author promotions, because it can be done on the cheap and can *potentially* reach lots of people. Authors I know are divided on the impact of these tours, but I find that they foster community among the authors and blogs involved, even if they don't lead to a significant rise in sales by themselves. I've paid for someone else to set up these tours, and have set them up myself (something Mark and I now do for many authors).

Do A Review Tour: One of my author friends says she no longer does blog tours, but instead does review tours, and works with a handful of reviewers who have proven that they review books fairly and aren't conduits to pirate sites. There are many shady reviewers out there, so it's important to try to work with those who care about what they do and who are above board. A strong review can help swing folks who aren't sure about taking a chance on your book, and many of these folks cross-post the reviews on Amazon and Goodreads.

Do Social Media: People on social media sites are often wary of blatant book promos. But there are still ways to promo yourself on social media without creating a backlash. Figure out what your favorite social media site likes and doesn't like. Find groups that include readers and writers in your genre and get involved. Find ways to be creative on social media, too. Instead of "buy my book," offer extra content on your blog—character pictures, cover reveals, exclusive excerpts, deleted scenes—things that can help prime the pump for your story.

Choose Your Cons: While you will probably never get the money back that you spend on a con in additional book sales, they are great places to a) meet your fans, b) network with other authors, and c) learn how others in the book industry do what they do. I especially like cons I can drive to, as it cuts out the cost of shipping books to the event.

Think Outside the Box: As I mentioned above, the thing that will most get people's attention for your book will be something they have never seen before. So be creative. Look at your work and think about what you could do to get it out there. Maybe some kind of unusual swag for the con? A crazy contest? Or dropping 100 copies from an airplane? Okay, maybe the last one is a bit over the top, and might generate a lawsuit or two (hey, they say no publicity is bad publicity, right?). But put your author mind to work and come up with something sublime.

Keep trying new things with each book release, and build on what you learn.

You never know what will click.

WRITING FOR A BLOG TOUR

One of the things that comes with being an author is promoting your work. A new release comes out, and you have to tell the world about it, so hopefully a few folks will want to give it a try.

Never mind that you've just read the bloody thing seventeen times in rough drafts and edits, and would sooner roll around in a bathtub full of fire ants than have to think about it or write about it again. You're probably going to have to do some kind of blog/review tour—whether you hire a company to handle it for you or do it yourself—and you're going to need to write some promotional blog posts.

So… what do you write about?

Here are a few things to try:

#ThrowbackThursday: People get a kick out of old photos of you, when you were still naive enough to believe that writing would bring you riches and fame. So dig into your old photo box or album, and pull out some *blog tour gold*. If it somehow ties into the theme or genre of your book, even better.

Inspiring Excerpt: Pick an excerpt that has a story tied to it—the bike ride you were on when the inspiration for that scene hit you. The thing your long-suffering spouse or precocious child said that made that scene click. The torrent of emotions that went into creating the scene in the first place. Give the audience a little *behind the scenes dirt*. They love that kind of thing.

Create a Playlist: Were there particular songs that helped you write the book? Or songs that fit certain scenes or moods of the story? Put together a playlist of these songs and share how and why they fit. Help the audience feel your pain. Or your joy.

The Extra Story Bit: Have any deleted scenes? These are great for sharing. "I wrote this scene and loved it, but then I cut it because it turns out my main character wasn't a Navy Seal after all." Alternately, write a flash fiction piece about one of the characters that reveals a little more about them. These are fun and add value to the story.

The Research: Did you go on a field trip to research the story? Use any special resources online? For one of my novellas, I took a trip to San Francisco with the honey to see what a thirty-foot rise in sea level would do to the city. The details I jotted down added a lot of richness and depth to the story that wouldn't have been possible otherwise.

The Interview: Many bloggers have a standard list of questions that they will send you upon request. These can be fun, and you don't have to think as much as when you write a post from scratch. But you can also do your own interview! Come up with five to ten questions, and then answer them yourself. I usually try to include a few writing process questions, a couple zingers that let you post fun and insightful answers ("tell me one thing hardly anyone knows about you" is one of my favorites), and a "what are you working on now" question. Have fun with it, and the audience will have fun too. Check the end of this book—there's a great list of author questions there for you to use.

Behind the Scenes—Writing: Take your audience on a little tour of how you came up with the story, or how it evolved—this can include an example of your first draft vs. your final draft of a particular paragraph; some insight that changed the story; or how a character evolved from draft to draft. Have a little fun with it.

Behind the Scenes—Cover: This is a really cool one to do. Share the evolution of your cover from start to finish, with photos (a slideshow is really great for this, if you have the capability). I have done this a number of times, and I really enjoyed showing how the cover went from a sketch to a finished product. If you used a cover designer, make sure you get their permission first.

Who Would Play My Characters in a Movie?: Let your imagination run wild. Choose your top two or three characters and find a movie star to fill the role. Fantasize a little about it. And who knows? Maybe one of your stars will read your post and want to do the movie, and you'll be plucked from relative obscurity to achieve the famous author status you so richly deserve. Hey, one can dream!

Not every blog tour post you write is going to be a magical work of art. Just do your best with the time you have, and try to enjoy it.

After all—this is your moment!

READING TO THE CROWD

The first time I read one of my works aloud, I was scared out of my mind.

Okay, that's not entirely true. The *first* time was a breeze. It was the second time that almost killed me.

The first time was at a small con in 2015. I was scheduled to read in a huge meeting room with at least a hundred chairs, and just looking at all of them made my heart beat like a jackhammer. But due to low con attendance and too much programming, I ended up reading to an audience of just six people—the four of us authors who were scheduled to read that hour, and two of our spouses. It was more of a love fest than an actual reading.

The second time was in front of a room full of people at a local library, and that was the really nerve-wracking one. There I was, book in hand, staring out at a bunch of strangers and daring to hold up my story as "art." What the hell was I thinking?

If you're an author, there's a better than even chance that you are not an accomplished public speaker. We tend to spend most of our time in our writing caves, and only come out when enticed by the smell of something delicious or the need to crash for a few hours of well-earned sleep.

As I have done more readings, I have learned a few things I hope will help make *your* reading a success:

Keep it Short: In my opinion, a good reading passage runs 5-7 minutes long—enough to hook the reader without leaving them glancing at their watches and looking longingly at the exit.

Choose Your Story Carefully: Generally speaking, I like to read my latest work, but that can vary. For a local bookstore reading, I read from a sci-fi novel that was far from my latest work, but it was the first book in the trilogy which included my latest one, so it seemed like a good place to start potential readers off with. On the other hand, I often read from *The River City Chronicles* for local events, as it has that hometown appeal.

Choose Your Reading Carefully: Good readings are focused—usually one to two characters—and if they have a high emotional content, so much the better. Also, readings that end at an interesting place—a cliffhanger, an emotional revelation, or a surprise—can leave your audience wanting more (and maybe get them to buy your book when the reading is over).

Practice it Four or Five Times: Read over it by yourself once or twice to get a feel for the meter of the piece, and where the emotional or action highs are. Then read it to someone else and get their reactions—how is your pacing? Is it a good choice for a reading? Anywhere they were confused? Finally, read it yourself a time or two more. You don't want to read it so many times that it becomes boring to you, but you do want to be familiar enough with it that you know where to pause, and where to punch the words for maximum effect.

Don't Be Afraid to Change the Words: A wise soul once told me that no one will ever go back and compare the words you read out loud to the ones on the page. Is there a word or phrase that you stumble over? Change it! A bit of foreshadowing that will have no impact on your current audience? Drop it! Some boring exposition that slows the action?

Cross it off. Make it easy to read, and it will flow better when you perform it at the reading.

Pack the Audience: Twist the arms of your friends and family to come to your reading so that a) worst case, you will have *someone* there, and b) best case, there will be friendly faces in the hopefully huge crowd. This will help your confidence enormously, especially when your super competitive sibling comes over with wide eyes to tell you, "I didn't know you had that in you!"

Set the Stage: Unless you are reading the first scene of the first chapter, you're likely dropping your audience in the middle of the river without a paddle—or even a canoe! Plan to give a short 1-3 sentence explanation of the book, and the characters and scene you are about to read.

Read From the Actual Book: If you can, read the text from your physical book. Sure, we all like to print out copies in Word that we can mark up and put into a bigger font. But there's just something wonderful and authentic about an author doing it the old-fashioned way, reading from a paperback copy of their own work.

Savor the Words: This was the hardest lesson for me to learn, but also the most important. My own tendency is to rush through things, to get them over and done with so I don't have to be in the hot seat anymore. This is a mistake. Your words have meaning, flavor, import. Slow down and feel them as you're reading. Find the heart of each sentence—is it comedy? Emotion? Action? And read it appropriately.

Don't be afraid to give a couple of seconds pause where needed. When you do it right, you can actually *feel* the connection with audience in every laugh, sigh, or smile. Remember, this isn't a sprint. It's a sharing, a gift you are giving to the audience.

Express Humility and Thankfulness: When you're done, you might feel ecstatic, or you might feel like you need to find the nearest bathroom to throw up. Or maybe both. Hold those emotions inside and *be there* for the people who gave up their plans to come see *you*. Some of them will want to speak to you, to ask questions, or tell you how much you touched them. Be humble, but not so humble that you won't accept their praise. It's their gift to you, another way for them to connect with you on a real and human level. And it's something you can use to keep you warm those long cold nights all alone inside your writer cave.

Reading in front of a crowd is a challenge, more so for some of us than for others. But it can also be one of the most rewarding aspects of this job. It's a chance for you to actually experience in real time the impact your words have on others.

So often we write in solitude, disconnected from the world by this screen in front of us. We put our stories out there and hope they find a home, that someone will take them in like a stray cat and give them the love we think they deserve.

A reading is one of those few times you can actually see it happen, right in front of you.

So the next time someone offers you the chance, take a deep breath, get yourself ready, and just do it.

PART SEVEN
GROUPS & EVENTS

Finding (or building) a writing community can help you immensely in the long run, giving you folks to bounce your ideas off of, beta readers, and partners for local events.

A LITTLE PHILOSOPHY: THE PINK FLOWER

had this weird dream.

I didn't remember much of it when I woke up, but one thing stood out—someone handing me a golf ball with a pink flower.

I'm sure this means little to you. You probably know nothing about golf balls, and if you do, a pink flower on one of them will likely have no significance for you.

I'm not a golf aficionado. My dad plays it, but it's never held much appeal for me. And yet, when I was in junior high, I flirted with sports, taking up tennis and then, for a very brief period, golf.

It's misleading to say Cross Junior High had a golf team. We had six or eight kids who came out to hit some balls around after school. The best of us even got to go out onto a *real* golf course now and then with our coach, while the rest hit balls at the driving range.

But we also practiced at the school, on a wide grassy lawn alongside one of the buildings. And in the sack of golf balls we used, there were dozens of standard white golf balls and one that had a single pink flower.

I don't know when it first happened, but at some point that ball became the most valuable one in the whole bunch.

We had these golf ball collector things—basically a long plastic tube that would suck up the balls we'd just hit out into the field—and as soon as we'd hit the last ball, we'd race out there as one with our collectors in hand, in search of the pink flower. And whoever found it would call out "got it!" in a triumphant yell.

Was there anything inherently better about that particular ball?

No.

Was it strange that a group of (supposedly) athletic guys in (fairly) repressive early eighties Arizona were excited by a pink flower?

Maybe.

But of course, it never was about the flower per se.

It was because it was *unique*.

As writers, we have an impossible task. We are usually also avid readers, and we have a body of work (in modern fiction) decades and decades long. We know from long experience that there is nothing new under the sun. And yet we are tasked with creating something shiny and moving and original, something unlike anything that anyone has ever read before.

And why?

Because people crave golf balls with pink flowers.

On an episode of the gay procedural drama "Instinct" with Alan Cummings, a singer killed himself because he had epilepsy-induced *Deja vu* that made everything around him, even his most original creative impulses, tired and unoriginal to him.

Can you imagine living in a world where nothing was ever new again?

That's what it's like, being an author. Our internal critic sits on our shoulders and lectures us about how derivative we are, how boring. How banal.

And yet we soldier on. We strive to create something impossible. We throw all the old pieces up in the air and hope they come down to us transformed.

And every now and then we succeed.

So the next time you find a pink flower while reading, celebrate it, and realize how unlikely its very existence is and how hard the author worked to make it blossom for you.

And if you manage to write one, throw up your hands in joy and dance under the silver light of the moon and stars.

MAKING CONNECTIONS

've been in the queer romance business now for six years, and the publishing biz for... well, let's just say quite a bit longer.

You can write a great novel. You can try to surf the latest trends. But the one thing you absolutely *have* to do if you want to be a successful author is make connections:

- Connections with readers who will love and recommend your books to others.
- Connections with publishers and/or vendors who will get the book out to those readers.
- Connections with other writers in your genre who will be your support system and shoulder to cry on.
- And connections with your community where, in time, you can become a beloved local writer.

All of this takes time, but it's really not that complicated: open yourself up to people around you, listen more than you speak, and give everyone you meet respect.

For example, in the last six years, I've made more than 4,000 friends on Facebook. The vast majority of these are simply passing sparks in the night, but at least five hundred are my core peeps—folks with whom I have carried on passionate conversations, consoled when publishers closed or a bad review came in, hugged at cons, and otherwise made strong and lasting connections.

These people cheer me on when a new story comes out, and they tell their peeps about me and it. And they hold my hand when I need to vent and scream and cry.

I'm embarking on a new phase of my career, taking my shot at the big leagues, but the game is still the same.

Connect, connect, connect.

And then repeat.

PREPARING FOR THE CON

One of the mainstays of the genre book business is the con. No, we're not talking about a complicated plot designed to illegally relieve someone of their hard-earned money. In this case, "con" is short for convention. They come in all sizes and flavors—there are huge romance cons, tiny sci-fi ones, and ComiCons in all shapes and forms.

A con is a great place to make contacts and get your name out there (and maybe even sell a couple books).

When preparing for a con, there's too much to do! It can be overwhelming, so I've made you a list of the most important things to do to prepare:

Book Your Hotel Early: Most of these cons offer a discounted hotel rate, but these often have limited availability. Book early to have the best shot at these low rates—otherwise it's going to cost you.

Pin Down Your Swag: Swag is that free stuff they give stars at the Oscars. It also refers to any promotional giveaway—bookmarks, buttons, pins, pens, and other materials authors use to promote their brand and their books. We can't all be as cool as my friend Angel Martinez and her anti-gravity cows, but you can come up with something perfect for your own books. Me, I like doing bookmarks (ordered from VistaPrint and paired with plastic holders and colorful yarn ties). Brainstorm and come up with something unique and cool.

Get Your Table Art: If you're going to have a table, you need to have something that shows folks who you are and what you do. I have a cool table runner with my author logo, and I usually put together some signage for the tabletop too. It makes you look professional, and can be re-used going forward for other cons.

Plan Your Weekend: When the con schedule comes out, sit down and spend a little quality time with it. Excel is your best friend here—I use it to make a schedule with dates and times and locations—but you can also fall back on a pad of paper. Whatever works for you. Figuring out which panels you're on, which ones you want to attend, and what else you want to do in advance can save you tons of heartache at the con, and can help you avoid double booking.

Get Your Books in Order: Which books will you take to sell at the con? How many are you likely to sell? Talk to other authors who have attended this particular con before to get an idea of how many copies you are likely to sell, and then figure out how to get them there. You can usually ship to the host facility, but then you run the risk of your stuff getting lost in the pile, and they often have strict (and short) delivery windows. If you know anyone in the area, see if they would be willing to take delivery for you and hold the books until you arrive.

Get Licensed: You may need a temporary local business license if you plan to sell books on-site. Contact the con organizers and/or the local city revenue division for more details.

Listen to Your Middle of the Night Voices: If you are like me, you get some of your best ideas in the middle of the night, when your writer brain wakes you up and tells you things that just couldn't wait until morning. For me, this applies to cons too. When this happens, get up and write down the ideas so a) you won't forget them, and b) tell your writer brain to shut the hell up and let you sleep.

Be Ready for the Emergencies: There *will be* unexpected twists and turns, crises, and emergencies at some point during the process—most likely the day before you head out to the con, or at the exact moment when you arrive. In my experience, books have been lost or misplaced, schedules changed at the last minute, and once I even forgot to make the hotel reservation. You can't plan for every possible contingency, but you can be ready to roll with things when they take a turn for the ridiculous, terrifying, or ugly. Remember, this too shall pass.

Give Yourself Some Play Time: You're in a new city, probably far away from where you live. Consider tacking on a day or two to your trip to see the local sites. Be a tourist—see the Liberty Bell, the Statue of Liberty, the world's largest ball of twine. It's all grist for your writing machine!

Figure Out Who Will Spell You for Bathroom Breaks: This is especially critical if you have a sales table at the con. Find someone who is willing to learn a little about your books and will sit in for you when you want to go see a panel, take a lunch break, or do those things we all need to do.

Attend to Your Personal Hygiene. Seriously: We all get wrapped up in our writing, sitting in our little writer caves, and many of us work a second (and sometimes third) job to pay the bills to allow us the ability to write. And it's easy to forget to comb your hair, put on clothes, and wear deodorant like a regular person every morning when you get up. So before you head off to the con, take a good look in the mirror and try to see yourself the way your fans will see you. If the sight of your unkempt self puts you off your breakfast, you may have some work to do.

Bone Up on Your Own Works: A true fan will know far more about your writing and your stories than you do. They have read each of them seven or eight times, and you just dashed the story off, stumbled through edits, and then never looked at it again.

So when they ask "Now in *Between the Lines*, on page 17 you said that Sam's mother lived in Tucson, but ten pages later, you suggest she actually lived in Central Arizona, and Tucson is in Southern Arizona. What did you really mean?" ... you need to be ready with an answer.

"Yes, she grew up in Tempe, a suburb just outside of Phoenix in CENTRAL ARIZONA, but when she was 18, she went for a degree in Astronomy to the University of Arizona in Tucson—in SOUTHERN ARIZONA—and never looked back."

Always Carry Your Own Pen: You never know when you may be asked for an autograph. You could be walking down the street when someone yells, "Hey Writer!" and you never know if they will have a pen handy. This has never actually happened to me. But I like to think that it could. So carry a reliable permanent marker at all times that will also work on skin, just in case your fans aren't carrying around a copy of your book when they run into you.

Be Humble: No one likes a prima donna writer. Have a series of humble phrases at hand at all times for when you are asked where your ideas come from or why you are such a great writer:

"Oh, I am just lucky to have been allowed to write for a living."

"I get my talent from my mother (God, the internet)."

"My success comes from my readers. Without them I would not exist."

But not too humble. No one likes a pushover. Be ready to defend your work if needed.

"Yes, I did really mean to make the sky red in my world."

"Yes, I really did count the number of steps in front of Capitol Hill."

And "No, I don't think Brad should have stayed with Jason. Jason was an asshole."

Remind Yourself Why You Write: This last one may be the most important of all. You got into writing for a reason. If you're like me, it's because you have an almost pathological NEED to write. And who do you write for? Your readers. You're here to see them, so enjoy it, and let them enjoy meeting you. A smile and a few friendly words cost you nothing.

When all is said and done, you're going to have a great time—you are going to a con with a bunch of friends and potential friends—people like you who do what you do or read it.

So take a deep breath, relax, and enjoy, and make notes for what to change the next time.

CREATING A LOCAL WRITING COMMUNITY

When I got serious about writing, I looked around for a local queer writing community here in Sacramento, and came up with nothing. Then one day, I had lunch with Pat and Christopher, two of my queer writer friends, and we decided to start one.

We've built a great, thriving local writer's group here in Sacramento with more than a hundred authors. We do local events together—Pride Festivals, book readings, and cons—and support one another when we need help.

So how do you build your very own local writers' group (for whatever your writing style and genre are)? I have some tips:

Find Your Core Group: What do you write? There are probably others in your community who write it too. Start with a few core folks who will help you build the group.

Reach Out to Other Local Authors: We pooled our resources and started reaching out to other local authors. We found them through a variety of means—friends of friends, Facebook, local events. We let bookstores and other community organizations (in our case, as a queer writers' group, the LGBT center and the Lavender Library) know we existed, and they have all funneled folks our way. And at almost every local event we find a couple more.

Pick a Regular Meeting Place: The core of our group is our bimonthly lunch—a chance for writers to hang out for a couple of hours, share tips, ask questions, and basically just enjoy the company of other authors. Find a central place with a good food section that has enough space for your group, and which is quiet enough for conversation.

Come Up With a Brand: Figure out a name for your group and delegate design of a logo to someone in the group who is good with graphic design. Delegation is key in these groups. Don't take it all on yourself or you *will* burn out, sooner or later. Once you have the design, you can get a table runner for any events your group may attempt. You can order one for about $37 (last time I checked) at a site like BannerBuzz.com, which you can use at local events. You'll also want to invest in a basic tablecloth to dress things up a bit.

Set Up Mentoring: One of my favorite things about our group is the capacity we have to help out new authors. We have a deep bench of experienced authors, and also some folks who are just getting started. We've been able to help many of them find their way, both in their writing and in getting published, both with one-on-one mentorships and general assistance from the group at large.

Find Community Events: One of the reasons for the existence of our group is to connect our authors with the greater local community. For us as an LGBTQ+ group, this comes in the form of attending gay pride events and doing readings at our local LGBT library. But it can also mean getting a table at your local farmer's market, or participating in a local book festival or other event. As a group, you can leverage your numbers to pay for tables, making such events much more affordable than doing it on your own. We don't collect annual dues, instead choosing to split costs on a per-event basis among attending authors.

Create a Mailing List: You can set up a free blog using any of a number of services—blogger.com, wordpress.com, etc. Once you have the site set up and a mailing plug-in chosen, you should start collecting names and emails for your list at the events you attend. Just make sure you get consent to be on your list—look up GDPR guidelines on Google for the strictest applicable law regarding this. We also created an eBook sampler of our works from a bunch of our authors that we provide for free to everyone who joins our list.

Be Creative: There are so many other ways you can grow your group and become a force for literature in your own community. Brainstorm with your members, and delegate. If someone has a great idea, ask them to run with it.

I'll be honest, creating a local group is hard, and it takes a lot of work to keep it going. Ours was sorely tested during the pandemic years, but has since bounced back to be better than ever.

And so many other local authors having your back is priceless.

RUNNING A GROUP SALES TABLE - PART 1: PLANNING FOR THE EVENT

N ow that you have a local network of authors, it's time to prepare for your first book selling event. When you're getting ready for it, there are a number of things you can do in advance to help it become a success. I'll share a few here:

Choosing the Event

As an LGBTQ+ group, our main focus is Pride events, but big city Prides can be quite expensive—way more than a typical author can afford. Your thing might be ComiCons, or local fairs, or even food and wine festivals. With the right planning, there are ways you can make even a fairly expensive event work.

First off, gauge interest in selling at the event among the writers in your local author community. In my experience, the optimal number of authors is 6, and probably 8 max for a 10 x 10 booth space. Find out what your author friends are willing to spend (per author), and that will give you an idea about what events you can afford. We typically target events that run $20-30 a person.

Second, find out what local events might be good venues for book sales, and make a list. Contact each of these, find out when vendor spaces go on sale and what they cost.

Finally, don't write off the big events. Yes, there are many more vendors, but also so many more people who are potential reader-buyers for your booth.

If the booth rate is over your budget, contact the organizer and explain that you are local authors (not deep-pocketed corporations) and ask if there is a discounted rate they might be able to offer you so that you can participate in the event.

Make sure you get firm commitments and payments from your authors before paying for the booth, and let them know their payments are non-refundable so you don't get left holding the bag if someone cancels. I also recommend adding a small amount to the per-author cost—this year we increased it by $5 per author—to help cover any unexpected events/needs. Any leftover money can go into your author group's fund for next time.

What You'll Need to Take

Make yourself a standard checklist of all the materials you will need at the event. At a minimum, I recommend:

- Your Books
- "Elevator Pitch" cards (to insert in each book with a catchy pitch that makes it easy for the reader to understand what your book is about)
- Book Stands (I love the fold-up wire ones)
- Removable Price Stickers
- Central Sales Method (PayPal/Zettle, Square, etc.—but be sure it takes credit cards and other electronic payment methods)
- External Battery and/or Extension Cord/Power Strip (depends on if your venue supplies electricity)
- Cash Box (with $200 in $1's, $5's and $10's)
- Canopy (for outdoor events—check and see if the event offers them first, and what they cost)

- Weights/Sandbags (in case it's windy)
- Tablecloth/Table Runner
- Large Binder Clips (to secure the tablecloth, unless you get one of those stretchy ones)
- Clipboard/Mailing List Sign-Up Sheet (be sure to follow GDPR protocols for getting reader permission)
- Pens
- Packing tape
- String/Cord
- Scissors/Boxcutter
- Swag
- Cooler with ice and water (for outdoor events)
- Snacks, Napkins, etc.
- Sunblock

Some optional add-ons:

- Tabletop Book Rack (to increase display space)
- Signage (a pop-up sign, a table runner, etc… Banner Buzz does nice runners fairly cheap)
- Folding Wagon (to haul the materials in)
- "Genre" Signs (especially if you have authors in a number of different genres)

All of these things cost money, but don't be intimidated. If it's your first time running a group table, use what you have. You can always add more as you go. For the larger purchases (canopy, signage, etc.), ask your group to chip in, with the understanding that it's a long-term investment that will benefit everyone.

Prepping for the Event

In the lead-up to the event, keep in regular touch with your participating authors. For our local Prides, we usually receive vendor information (rules, suggestions, booth location/map, etc.) a week or two before the event. Rather than making the authors wade through it all, I have a standard email template I send them that summarizes the important info—what I will be handling, what they need to prepare, their expected booth responsibilities, the drop-off time and location details, etc.

We expect all of our authors to arrive about an hour before opening for set-up. We do a short training on the sales system, and expect everyone to know how to run it. During the event, it's quite common to have one author running the sale while the selling author talks to the reader and signs their book, so everyone needs to know how to use it.

We also ask that everyone clearly price their books in flat $ amounts, using removable labels on the bottom right corner of each copy of their books. Keeping the labeling consistent makes it easier on the booth visitor.

We collect taxes inclusive of the cover price (i.e., we don't add it on top), so all sales come out in flat dollar amounts. This makes it much easier to run cash sales, as there's no coin change involved. But because the tax will be taken off the cover sales price, we recommend that our authors add a $1 or so to their pricing to make up for it. These taxes and the Paypal fees will be deducted from each sale before the earnings are sent to the author after the event.

You may also want to scope out the parking situation and local food options before you go, unless you plan to pack a lunch.

The Paperwork

There's one more thing you need to do before the event, and I'd recommend tackling it a couple months early—get your tax and business license paperwork in order. In California, we generally need two official pieces of paper to sell books at these events:

City Business License: Contact the event organizers or the revenue department in your host city and find out their requirements, Generally speaking, this will run around $20, and may be an annual license or a temporary/event one. That cost should be added to your table cost and shared among all participating authors.

State Event Permit (Sales Tax): It may work slightly differently in your area, but if your state has a sales tax, you generally need to report that you will be selling at the event to your state sales tax department. In CA, it's the California Department of Tax and Fee Administration (CDTFA). I have an account there, and I login to create an "event" for each Pride we're selling at. In January, I report the income for each event and the taxes collected, and pay them to the state (which distributes a portion to each city).

One more tip: When setting up your payment equipment, be sure you get the local tax rate right for each event in the system, so you don't end up owing more or less tax than you collect.

If it seems like a lot, well, it is. But start small and take it a step at a time.

After a few of these, you'll be a pro!

RUNNING A GROUP SALES TABLE - PART 2: THE PREGAME AND THE EVENT ITSELF

We've covered the prep for your first big shared-author event. So what happens when it's boots on the ground?

The Pregame

I always try to reconfirm with everyone the week before the event. Just a quick message, text, or email asking them to get back to me and let me know it's still a go (and confirm that they have paid their share).

The day before the event, I go through my checklist one last time, and make sure everything is accounted for. I also pack it all into the car so there's no rush in the morning (that's when I tend to forget the important things).

We have a really cool foldable metal bookstand that greatly increases the display space on our table. One year at a local event half an hour away from home, I forgot to take it, and Mark had to make the hour-long round-trip to get it (bless his heart). After the *incident,* he made me make a checklist for all the materials we would need.

I also recommend planning for breakfast and lunch beforehand. Are you going to grab something on the way or eat at home? Are you counting on food trucks for lunch? Who knows what will be there? And long lines may mean precious selling time away from your table. Or will you eat locally, or even take your lunch? If you plan to eat out, try to figure out where and how to get there in advance, and confirm that they will be open that day.

Make sure everyone has your cell phone number and vice versa, both to check in when folks are late arriving and in case they need to reach you at lunch if you leave the booth.

I recommend that you ask for everyone to be there an hour before start time. It always takes longer than you think it will to set things up, and you'll want a little time to go over procedures with your table mates before the gates (or doors) open.

The Payment System

What you use for payment will vary, but there are a few things that are universal.

First off, if you plan to only take cash, you're cutting off a large number of potential sales. At our most recent events, about 20% paid in cash. If it was the only option, some folks who preferred credit would probably still come up with the cash to make the purchase, but you're probably leaving 50-60% of your potential sales on the table if you don't take credit cards.

We use a card processor app for running transactions. One advantage is that it also allows us to take Venmo, PayPal and Apple/Android payments, so there's no excuse for folks not to buy.

I highly recommend going through the process at home yourself. Write up a "how-to" sheet that the others manning the booth can refer to when you are away (remember that lunch thing we talked about?). If you're using a tablet or smart phone as your processing device (with a card reader), make sure it's not password protected so your booth authors don't accidentally get locked out when you're gone.

Most payment systems will let you input items ahead of time, to make it easy to select them when a customer purchases them, but for our purposes, I've found this is not practical. It either requires me to have everyone submit all the books they plan to bring with prices beforehand, and then take a lot of my time to enter them, or try to do it all in the rush of the morning.

Instead, we simply have each author enter the info on the fly. If an author buys a copy of my book *The Stark Divide*, Grete's *Chlorophobia*, and Marvin's *Contact*, whoever processes the sale enters those three books as temporary items into the payment system.

It doesn't matter if some people use a partial title, or add the "The" at the end. I clean that up when I download the sales report after the event.

In practice, we've turned into a well-oiled machine—the author(s) who sell their books generally sign them for the customer while one of the other folks in the booth runs the sale and offers a bag.

Some author groups opt to have each individual author run their own sales with their own equipment. This is fine... but we've found that making it easier on folks to buy multiple authors' titles can also increase overall sales, and decrease "friction" for your customers.

Table Layout

We used to organize books on the table by author name, but recently we've switched to the "bookstore" model—we have tags for each genre (preprinted, and a few blanks just in case) and we arrange the books under those genre categories. This makes it easier to direct folks to whichever genre(s) they are looking for.

Have your authors tell each other what they write before things get started, and make sure each author has their "elevator pitch" cards written out and inserted in the top/front copy of each title. As the day goes on, you'll each figure out the other's books, and be ready to make recommendations of your fellow authors' works:

"Like space opera? Check out Scott's Ariadne Cycle series here."

"Paranormal? Oooh, Marvin has a cool book about vampires and werewolves on the moon right here."

Be generous with your recommendations—remember, they're going to be the ones recommending your books when you're out at lunch.

The Pitch

The single best thing we've all learned to do to make sales and find more local readers for our books is the reader sales pitch. It's super simple:

"What do you like to read?"

We ask this of folks browsing the table, and folks walking by who give the books a glance. It often works to bring them over and get them engaged.

Once we know what they like, we direct them to that section of the table, and "tap in" the appropriate authors to talk to them.

Our superpower is that we're not just a bookstore with an uninterested clerk trying to sell them something. We're the *actual authors*—and people's eyes often go wide when they realize that they're talking to the folks who wrote these books. There's a mystique around talking to *real authors*, and we utilize it to the fullest.

Don't get me wrong. It's not *just* a sales thing. We're also thrilled to make someone's eyes light up, and to tell them about what we've written.

Next time you're selling books at an event, give it a try. It really works.

Don't Forget the Newsletter List

Everyone who comes to your table should be directed to sign up for your mailing list, either after they make a purchase or in lieu of one if they seem disinclined:

"Would you like to join our email list? That way we can let you know when we're doing future events."

These are book lovers who live near you—you want them on your list!

We share the list with the participating authors. We let them know this up front, and include a GDPR (the European privacy law) notice at the bottom of each sheet:

By signing up on this form, I agree to be added to ORGANIZATION NAME's and the participating authors' email lists. ORGANIZATION

NAME/the authors will send me periodic info, news, events, and offers. I can be removed from these lists at any time by clicking on the unsubscribe link on any of the emails, or by replying and requesting removal. My email won't be shared with anyone else without my explicit prior approval.

There's also a checkbox for "author" in case the person signing up is a writer interested in joining the group—I make sure this gets checked off for any new authors who sign up.

We also usually give away a free eBook to everyone who joins—I send this out after the event.

It's a Group Effort

I regularly run across readers looking for sci-fi and fantasy—my jam. I could just direct them to my books—after all, I want to sell the most, right? But I always include one of mine and at least one of the other authors who sell that genre at the table.

Why?

Because you don't know what flavor of the reader's preferred genre might click with them best. And because we're all in it together. We want all of us to be successful, so they'll want to do this again next year. And when I'm away from the booth, I know they will sell my books too.

There's no room for ego at one of these events.

Packing Up

Everything must come to an end. But when? Most events have a posted start and end time, but it's not uncommon for vendors to start packing up when things slow down.

Unfortunately, this usually starts a stampede for the exits.

Check your event's vendor info—do they require you to stay until a set time before you are allowed to pack up?

We tend to err on the conservative side. We don't usually put our books away until about half the booths are around us are empty, and sometimes we've made some nice last-minute sales as a result.

We ask everyone to stay until the end if possible, which makes the wrap-up go faster.

After the Event

Once the event is over, I get home and clear out the car. If I have another event in the near future, I leave the removable price labels on my books; if not, I take them off, because even "easy remove" labels can degrade and cause issues over time.

Then I download the PayPal/Zettle sales report (or whatever payment app you use). I clean up the book titles so they're uniform, then add a column to calculate sales tax.

One note: we do all our pricing "tax inclusive," meaning we choose flat dollar amounts (ie: $10.00) and then pay the tax out of that amount on the back end. One thing that threw me off: Let's say the tax is 10%. 10% on $10.00 is $1.00. But 10% on $9.10 (the original $10 minus the tax you are paying) works out to just 9.1 percent of the $10. Confused? I was too.

So if I take $10 and ADD a 10% tax on top, that's $11.00.

But when I make the $10 tax inclusive, I'm really selling the book for $9.10 with .91 tax (10%). So if I want to calculate the tax off the original amount paid by the customer, I'm going to multiply that $10 (in this example) by 9.1%, not 10%.

This is basically a long-winded way of saying "remember to base your tax calculation on the price you sold the book for minus the tax."

Once I have everything added in, I create a simple version of my spreadsheet with Author, Title, Price, PayPal Fee, Tax, and Net Amount columns, sort it by author and book, total up each of their fields, and send it to the group.

I also confirm that the cash received matches what the payment system thinks we sold.

Once everything is deposited in the bank account we use, I issue PayPal, Venmo or check payments to the table share authors, depending on their preference (Venmo and checks do not charge an extra fee).

I also send the authors the mailing list sign-ups, with a recommendation that they email the list once first and explain why they are being added to that author's list, and give them a chance to decline. And I send the new sign-ups a free eBook as a thank you, and contact any new authors with steps to join.

When all of that's done, you're ready to start it all over again for the next event!

I find these events very rewarding, and the sales are nice too. They help you build up your local author network, and may bring you additional opportunities and new members.

I hope you try it, find great success, and most importantly, have fun.

PART EIGHT
REVIEWS & REALITY CHECKS

And finally, what we all have to deal with (and wish we didn't)—the critics (both internal and external) that are the bane of every writer.

A LITTLE PHILOSOPHY: SMALL JOYS

Being a writer is a lonely profession. Most of your time is spent in front of your computer, alone, trying to spin words into worlds and fighting off those dreaded twin feelings of fraud and failure.

So when something good happens, even if it's just a "small joy," you have to learn to embrace it, and use it to feed your writing soul.

Like when one of your stories is rejected by an editor you submitted it to, but the email is accompanied by a very nice note saying that they hope it will find a home elsewhere. Grieve the rejection, but celebrate the feedback. Then turn it around to the next place on your list.

Which then rejects it within hours. Not only that, but they include a personal note that you forgot to double space the manuscript. *Gah.*

You *should* be devastated, right? Two rejections in less than twenty-four hours, *and* a stupid rookie mistake?

But think about what that comment means. They actually *looked* at your story. They considered it, and you have the *proof.*

Think of all those small joys we as writers experience, and how they can help light the way for us even when things seem bleak, if we let them.

A few of mine:

- The first time someone came up to me at a con and told me they absolutely loved one of my stories, and how excited they were to see me there.
- Those moments when the story you've been fighting with suddenly clicks, and everything just falls into place.
- Getting my author copy in the mail, and putting it up on my author shelf.
- When someone tags me on Facebook as "the guy who writes that thing you are looking for."
- When my husband Mark turns to me after finishing a beta read and says, "I think that's the best thing you've ever written."
- When I type those magical two words (even if it's just in my head, because, who really ever includes them anymore?) "The End."

There *are* joys in writing, both large and small, but the small ones come more often. Celebrating them will help sustain you until the next one arrives.

So acknowledge them when they happen, and use them to fuel your work.

One of my favorite lines from the U.S. version of *Queer as Folk* applies here:

"Mourn the losses because they are many. But celebrate the victories, because they are few."

THE WAITING GAME

I t's something every author has to learn to do—to wait gracefully for a response after submitting a story to a publisher or an agent.

I am calm.
I am relaxed.
I am TOTALLY FREAKING OUT AND WHY HAVEN'T THEY GOTTEN BACK TO ME... DO THEY HATE ME? AM I A HORRIBLE WRITER? WHAT IS WRONG WITH ME?
takes deep breath
I am calm. I am relaxed.

I won't lie to you. It sucks. Almost as bad as when you finally get a reply email and open it, heart pounding, only to find it's another rejection.

As you become more experienced at your craft and the whole submissions thing, you learn a few things about the process, and may be able to approach it a little more calmly. So here are my suggestions:

Confirm Receipt: When you submit your story, ask for a receipt confirmation in your email. If it's one of those auto submission sites, make note of the confirmation number and status website. That way you'll know they got it, instead of waiting for a couple months, only to find out that the file went to their spam folder and you either missed a deadline or have to start waiting all over again.

It Takes As Long as It Takes: You can't rush these things. The publisher will get back to you when they are ready. And sure, we all want to get that exciting email—"your story was so amazing that we just had to tell you right away!" But most of the time, you won't get an answer until the last possible moment.

Desperation is Not Pretty: You should never bug the editor before the stated deadline for a response, and you most certainly should *never, ever* scream, yell, or cry in your emails to them. Once the deadline has passed without a response, if I still haven't gotten a response, I send one very polite and friendly email, just to be sure it's still in queue.

Be Graceful in Defeat: Editors and publishers are people too, and they know what they are looking for that will suit their anthology or product line. If your story isn't it, it's usually not personal. When I am rejected, I send a quick "thanks so much for considering me" response and leave it at that. Don't burn bridges you may need later. I have a few close friends to whom I can grumble to my heart's content about the unfairness of the world at large and publishing in particular. I NEVER direct those sentiments to the editor or publisher, or put them out in public.

Rejection is an Opportunity: It's true. There are so many publishers these days, and self-publishing has become much easier. Keep a list of possible publishers, and when that manuscript comes back to you, send it out into the world again and again until you find it a good home. And if all else fails, you can put it out into the world yourself.

Celebrate the Wins: The first short story I published netted me $35. Mark and I went out to dinner that night and spent almost $100. I'm not advocating that you blow all your royalties on steak and lobster, but these things happen rarely enough that it's important to do something nice to mark the occasion. It will help tide you over, the next time you get rejected.

How you handle waiting and rejection is at least as important as how you handle success. Keep yourself busy while you wait—what's the next thing you wanted to write?

And if a rejection does finally come, take it in stride and keep moving.

F@CK THE REVIEWS

Sometimes when you think you have this whole writer gig figured out, life steps in to give you a hard slap across the cheek.

A couple years into my writing career, I ran across a review that was so negative it might have stopped my nascent writing career in its tracks if I had seen it when it was first published, soon after I started writing seriously. I patted myself on the back for being so much more evolved these days, both in writing skill and in my reaction to my sometimes-bad reviews.

I'd even half-convinced myself that I was past the whole negative review phase of my writing career. That from here on out, it would be sunshine and puppies and smooth sailing on the reviews front.

Then I found a new review in a trade magazine for one of my latest books, and it was devastating. *Too choppy, poor world-building, sketchy characters.*

Bad world-building? That's my jam!

I'm not going to name the reviewer here. Most reviewers do what they do for the love of reading and for little or no money, and I can't fault them for expressing their honest opinions about my work, even when it hurts.

Instead, I want to talk about our relationship to reviews as authors.

As a newbie author, most of us are told the same thing. Don't read your reviews on reader sites. Several of them are known haunts for review trolls—people who post negative reviews with the sole aim of hurting the author and/or provoking a reaction.

But it's not quite so simple as "never read your reviews." If you're lucky, your book will get picked up by professional reviewers and trade magazines—folks whose job it is to give their opinions about the books they read. These are (generally) marked by a higher standard of critique than your standard reader review, and can be influential in helping to sell your book. If a reviewer loves it, some of their readers may become your readers.

As an author, you may find it necessary to read these professional reviews of your work, as a) they may be raves, and useful in marketing your release, and b) they come from people whose opinions you generally respect.

Every author gets bad reviews, just like every author gets rejections—even the rich and famous ones did, before they struck it big.

But reviews are different, somehow. Unlike publisher rejections, negative reviews generally go into excruciating detail about what the reviewer did not like about your book.

It's as if someone took your baby and said, "He's too short. His hair isn't blond enough, his teeth are crooked, and I don't like the way he looks at me when I pick him up. Oh, and what's that awful smell?"

It *feels* personal.

But here's the thing. Generally it's not. Usually the reviewer has a stack of books, and they are hoping with all their heart that the next book they pick up will make their soul sing, their imagination fly, and their thoughts return to your story again and again for weeks after they complete the review.

Then they read your book, and for whatever reason it doesn't click with them. And it's their job to explain why.

So how do you react when you get one of these takedowns of our work?

You cry. Of *course* you do. Someone just punched your baby, and it *hurts*.

You share it with a close friend or two, and commiserate about what a dark and awful world you live in, where no one appreciates your raw talent and sterling storytelling ability (this despite the fact that you got five glowing reviews of your work the day before the bad one).

Then you move on.

Never get in a fight with a reviewer or a fan. I can't emphasize this one enough, and I am deadly serious about it. If someone disses you, or gives you a terrible review online, *do not engage.* You will *always* lose. Even if you win, you will lose. The internet is not kind to authors who take down people who don't like their work.

Instead, calmly shut down your computer. Walk into the most private room in your house—the bathroom will do nicely for this. Run all the taps. Then scream at the top of your lungs for five minutes. Once you're done, take a cough drop for your sore throat, and go out to your favorite coffee shop for a latte.

I *never* respond directly to a bad review. I have too much respect for the folks doing the reviewing, and even if I didn't, if I had reason to suspect that a reviewer was out to get me, no good would come of it. We live in a small, beautiful publishing ecosystem, and the author that starts attacking reviewers willy-nilly is not long for the reviewing world.

But there is one more thing you *should* do, one that I think is vital to becoming a better writer. I've long said that once you decide you know all there is to know about writing, your own work stagnates and ceases to grow.

Bad reviews are like a fire burning through an old forest, causing rack and ruin, but also creating rich soil and letting in the light so new things can grow. Remember how I said writing was like a garden? Sometimes it needs to be reduced to ash to make the soil fertile again.

Sit with your negative review for a while. Let it roll around in your subconscious, and you may start to understand (if not actually agree with) some of the things your reviewer said.

Taking the time to absorb what the reviewer said instead of rejecting it outright may push you down the path of personal writing growth.

In my early reviews, reviewers generally cited two main deficiencies in my writing—a lack of good character building and growth, and the fact that my works were too short.

So I studied other works and read books about character development and taught myself how to write better characters. And I took the second complaint as a compliment—they wanted more!—and started writing novels instead of novellas, giving my ideas more room to roam.

And guess what? My reviews got better.

So next time you get a negative review, get a pint of Ben and Jerry's and have a good cry with a friend or two. And then start plotting your revenge.

Teach yourself how to write better.

IMPOSTER OR BUST

When we left home for my first WorldCon, I felt pretty good about myself. I'd published over twenty stories, including four novels with three more on the way. I'd gotten great reviews, and my publisher at the time seemed to like me. Sure, I wasn't big money yet, but was on my way.

Right?

Then I got to WorldCon.

There were close to 4,000 people there. I think half of them were authors, and every single one seemed younger and more creative than me:

- Astrophysicists who were also authors, and had the physical science stuff down cold.
- Writers who had been perfecting their craft for thirty years, who were roughly my age.
- Newbies who had stories in consideration for Hugo awards.

Suddenly I felt like a rank amateur, someone who didn't know what the hell he was doing.

Then I met an author who has done what no one else has done before —won the Hugo Award for three years running.

I felt like such an imposter.

Every writer goes through this now and then—there's even a name for it. It's called (wait for it) Imposter Syndrome.

As an author, you reach a certain level of success and look around, and wonder who the hell let you into this little club, what they were smoking, and how long it will take before somebody figures out that you don't belong and kicks you out.

It doesn't take much to tip you from confidence in your writing skills into a savage conviction that you should never be allowed to write again. One bad review. One fantastic book that seems so much better than any of the dreck we write. One other author who seems to have it all.

And there you are, tumbling into the abyss once more.

So what do you do?

Sit back, and take a big breath.

Remind yourself that you write because you *love* doing writing, because you *need* to. Remember that each of those other authors has felt the same thing at one point or other. And remember that when you stop feeling this way, when you think you know it all, you stop learning, and your writing stagnates.

I may not know you, but I bet you're pretty good at this "telling stories" thing. You cared enough about your writing to pick up this book in the hopes that it would help you get better. All you can do is write the best story you can, each time, and try to learn how to write even better the next time around.

One of the panels at WorldCon was called "You Do Belong Here." I think I'm going to make that my new mantra.

This is my club, too. I *do* belong here.

And so do you.

WHAT WE DO MATTERS

I'm a writer because I need to write. I have things to say, and I wasn't gifted enough (or maybe in the right way) to express them through acting, art, or music, and so I write.

Most days, writing is a strictly solitary sport, practiced in a dark room staring at a bright screen. We do it because we love it, because we need it, and because when we don't do it, something doesn't feel right.

And then we wrap up our little word babies and set them adrift on the river, hoping someone downstream picks them up and gives them love and finds a little joy in the process.

Armisted Maupin said it well in his Afterword for *Tales of the City*:

"When a novel has survived for twenty years, it's virtually on its own. It goes gallivanting all over the place without so much as a postcard home to its bewildered parent. Royalty sheets can offer some clues as to its whereabouts, but not the sort of vivid details the author really cares about."

While my novels haven't been around for twenty years (yet) and haven't seen anywhere near the levels of success that Maupin's have, I know what he's getting at here. As artists, we crave the reaction to our art, and it's rare that we actually get it.

Sometimes though, we get lucky.

I wrote a novella called *Slow Thaw* for Mischief Corner Books' holiday collection one year, a gay/trans love story set in one of the harshest locations on Earth—Antarctica. And it's also about climate change. Adding that element was an intentional choice, but not one I was sure would be welcomed in the greater world.

I feel I have a responsibility as an author—especially as a sci-fi author—to make the warning bells ring far and wide as I see us slipping into deeper and deeper danger. And a large part of this is due to both climate change and to the climate change deniers, egged on by Big Oil and their friends. It's a bad habit we're hooked on, and like many street drugs, it's eventually going to kill us.

Then I started getting reviews like this one:

"I enjoyed this book, but the happily ever after didn't take away the grim message about what we're doing to this planet and how irreversible the damage may be, and sooner than we think."

And this one:

"It's a tale that I'm glad I read as it's made me focus again on 'green' stuff that is in the back, not the forefront, of my mind, and yes it needs to be in the latter. No, I'm not about to become an activist! but I will try more to do my bit for the planet."

And this one:

"A fast-paced romance set in Antarctica. Unfortunately it was very realistic portrayal of what could be a testament to the perils we face due to climate change! A fact too many politicians refuse to accept."

Sure, I don't have a huge platform like Stephen King or Armisted Maupin. But what I wrote made a difference in these three people's lives and perceptions, and I'm sure in many more who didn't take the time to leave a review.

Something to remember the next time I sit down in front of my keyboard to write.

What we do as writers matters, and it can change the world in ways small and large.

That's why I wrote this book. It came about in an unconventional fashion, as blog posts over almost a decade on my writing blog. As I navigated the indie author and small press world, I've learned a lot, and I've been fortunate enough to have a small platform from which to share those ideas and lessons with my writing friends.

So I hope you keep this book handy to guide you on your own journey through the wilds of indie publishing.

Keep writing.

—J. Scott Coatsworth

WHY I WROTE THIS BOOK

I've been writing professionally since 2014. I've published ten novels, eight novellas, thirty-two short stories and twelve multi-author anthologies. I've also written over 400 weekly columns for my blog, discussing many of the things I've learned as an indie author.

I've been an avid reader since I was a little kid. When I was in my early elementary school years, my Mom started me on the Lord of the Rings, and I fell in love with science-fiction and fantasy.

I was forty-five when I finally started writing professionally. Within a year, I'd sold a few novellas and short stories, and a couple years later, I sold my first two novels, both the starts of series—*Skythane* and *The Stark Divide*, my prequel novel. Since then, I have had my books published with a number of small and mid-sized presses.

In short, I love everything about publishing.

In 2018, I decided to venture out into indie publishing for the first time. I was so scared when I pressed the "submit" button on my first indie book on the Amazon website. I knew *nothing* about being an indie author *or* self publishing, and I was certain I was going to do it all wrong.

And I did.

But that's part of the journey. You're going to make mistakes, and that's okay. Each one is a learning experience—a chance to do it right the next time.

I was lucky. I had a wonderful group of authors in my friend circle who had gone through all of this before.

Bit by bit, by trial and error and calling in a lot of favors, I figured out how to upload my books to each of the book sales platforms. I upped my game with my writing craft, and figured out which parts of the indie author job I could do myself and which I needed to hire others to help me with. I slowly grew my press, Other Worlds Ink, and kept learning about what it meant to be an indie author, what it required of me, and how to survive the ups and downs it inevitably brings.

As I learned, I chronicled what I found on my blog, and those posts became the basis for this book.

I don't claim to have all the answers. There's always more to learn, and things in the indie publishing world are constantly changing.

What I can do is hold out a hand, help you find your own path, and give you a virtual hug when things go awry.

I hope this book has inspired you to pick up your pen and scribble out all the wonderful stories dancing in your brain, and that it helps you figure out what to do with them next.

Being an indie author is an ongoing journey, and there's always something new to learn. It will can take you amazing places, if it doesn't kill you first (spoiler alert: it probably won't).

And build your writing community. We're all in this together.

AUTHOR INTERVIEW QUESTIONS

Another great source for blog tour content is the author interview. It's a pull-back-the-curtains thing that lets your readers (and potential readers) get to know you a little better.

Here's my list of suggested interview questions for creating blog tour content. I suggest taking five or six of these at a time, from the various lists, and making a unique guest post out of them. I also recommend that you include this one at the end of each interview:

What are you working on now, and when can we expect it?

Here are the rest of the questions. Feel free to modify them or add your own.

Writing Questions:

When did you know you wanted to write, and when did you discover that you were good at it?

If you could sit down with one other writer, living or dead, who would you choose, and what would you ask them?

How would you describe your writing style/genre?

What was your first published work? Tell me a little about it.

What's the weirdest thing you've ever done in the name of research?

Have you ever taken a trip to research a story? Tell me about it.

What is your writing Kryptonite?

What do you do when you get writer's block?

Do you use a pseudonym? If so, why? If not, why not?

If you could tell your younger writing self anything, what would it be?

Do you ever base your characters on real people? If so, what are the pitfalls you've run into doing so?

How long do you write each day?

Do you reward yourself for writing, or punish yourself for failing to do so? How?

Do you read your book reviews? How do you deal with bad or good ones?

How long on average does it take you to write a book?

What do you do if you get a brilliant idea at a bad time?

Why did you choose to write in your particular field or genre? If you write more than one, how do you balance them?

How long have you been writing?

Are there underrepresented groups or ideas featured in your book? If so, discuss them.

Are you a full-time or part-time writer? How does that affect your writing?

Are you a plotter or a pantser? Or...?

Do your books spring to life from a character first or an idea?

How did you deal with rejections?

How long does it take you to write the first draft?

What is the most heartfelt thing a reader has said to you?

What tools do you feel are must-haves for writers?

What was one of the most surprising things you've learned in writing your books?

Where do you like to write?

What are your favorite parts of publishing?

What are your least favorite parts of publishing?

What advice do you wish you'd had before releasing your first story?

If you had a grant to write any book you wanted as a freebie without worrying about sales, what kind of story would you like to tell?

How do you approach cover art for your indie stories?

What was the most valuable piece of advice you've had from an editor?

Name the book you like most among all you've written, and tell us why.

How do you combine all the different worlds of your life in your works?

What's the funniest or creepiest thing you've come across while researching for one of your stories?

What's your writer cave like? Photos?

What does success mean to you?

What book is currently on your bedside table?

About Your Book:

How did you choose the topic for this book?

Tell us something we don't know about your heroes. What makes them tick?

Tell us one thing about them that we don't learn from the book, the secret in their past.

What were your goals and intentions in this book, and how well do you feel you achieved them?

What was the hardest part of writing this book?

Who did your cover, and what was the design process like?

What question do you wish that someone would ask about your book, but nobody has? Write it out here, then answer it.

What character gave you fits and fought against you? Did that character cause trouble because you weren't listening and missed something important about them?

What inspired you to write this particular story? What were the challenges in bringing it to life?

What secondary character would you like to explore more? Tell me about them.

Who has been your favorite character to write and why?

What was the weirdest thing you had to Google for your story?

What's your core motivation in writing this book?

Let's talk to your characters for a minute – what's it like to work for such a demanding writer?

Are you happy with where your writer left you at the end? (don't give us any spoilers).

Personal Questions:

As a child, what did you want to be when you grew up?

If you had the opportunity to live one year of your life over again, which year would you choose, and why?

Tell me one thing hardly anyone knows about you.

Tell me about a unique or quirky habit of yours.

Were you a voracious reader as a child?

What pets are currently on your keyboard, and what are their names? Pictures?

What's your writing process?

What was the first book that made you cry?

What other artistic pursuits (if any) do you indulge in apart from writing?

What are some day jobs that you have held? If any of them impacted your writing, share an example.

We know what you like to write, but what do you like to read in your free time, and why?

What qualities do you and your characters share? How much are you like them, or how different are they from you?

Fun Questions:

Describe yourself using... (choose one: a food, a book, a song, a movie, an animal, a drink, a place, etc.)

Do you have any strange writing habits or superstitions?

If you could create a new holiday, what would it be?

If you were stuck on a desert island all alone with only three things, what would they be?

What action would your name be if it were a verb?

What fantasy realm would you choose to live in and why?

What speculative fiction character would you like to spend an evening with, and why?

Which of your own characters would you: Kill? F@ck? Marry? And why?

Would you visit the future or the past, and why?

How does the world end?

Star Trek or Star Wars? Why?

What meds are you supposed to be taking?

What's your drink of choice?

What's in your fridge right now?

What food(s) fuel your writing?

If you could choose three authors to invite for a dinner party, who would they be, and why?

Would you rather be in a room full of snakes or a room full of spiders?

What's your favorite line from any movie?

Do you believe in love at first sight?

RECOMMENDED RESOURCES

I thought I'd include a few resources here for indie authors that might help you on your journey.

Other Books About Writing:

- *The Art of Character*, by David Corbett
- *Crafting Category Romance*, by Amy Lane
- *Telling Writing*, by Ken Macrorie
- *Write Characters Your Readers Won't Forget*, by Stant Litore
- *Writing Down the Bones*, by Natalie Goldberg

Writing & Series Bible Apps

- Campfire is a world-building/series bible app that helps you "overcome disorganization," according to their website.
- Dabble is a writing app that purports to be a little simpler than Scrivener.
- One Note is Microsoft's note-taking app that also allows you to add other media (pictures, videos, etc.). Similarly, some folks use Evernote.
- Scrivener offers an immersive writing app that will keep track of the details for you, but has a lot of moving parts.

Websites:

- BookBub: A daily newsletter for special book deals
- BookBrush: A website that allows you to make book covers and banners without buying an expensive graphics app
- Bookshop.org: An online site that specializes in selling print books and funneling the sales to independent bookstores
- BookFunnel: An author service that specializes in ebook and audio distribution, sending ARCs

- Canva: A browser-based graphic design app that includes free and paid options
- Deposit Photos: A stock photo site that lets you use their images on book covers with a standard license (up to 500,000 copies in print, unlimited in eBook distribution)
- Draft2Digital: This is a book distribution for indie authors and small presses which is also useful for making free downloadable eBooks out of Word files
- OtherWorldsInk: Our author services company and publisher, specializing in blog tours, book formatting, and cover wraps for print books
- ProlificWorks: A site for teaming up with other authors for book giveaways
- SFWA's Indie Author 101 Section: The Science Fiction & Fantasy Writers Association maintains a great section with lots of general info for indie authors on publishing and marketing your book
- StoryOrigin: A site that specializes in facilitating book mention swaps in author newsletters, among other author services
- VistaCreate (formerly Crello): Another online graphic design site, now owned by VistaPrint
- William Shunn's Formatting Guides: Widely accepted as the industry standard for preparing your manuscript for submission to an agent or editor.

Swag & Con Supplies:

- Banner Buzz: Great for tablecloths and table runners with your logo, among other types of banners
- Just Buttons: My go-to for button swag
- Vista Print: My go-to for postcards, bookmarks, business cards —basically any printed paper. They do T-shirts too. They have regular sales and special offers, so get on their mailing list ad watch for one a few months before your next in-person event

GLOSSARY

Accomplishments List: A list of all the things we've accomplished as writers during our careers.

Advance: Short for an *advance on royalties*, an amount some publishers pay an author when buying their book. Actual royalties are deducted from this amount until it is "paid off."

Advance Review Copy (ARC): An almost-finished version of your book —usually created at the end of the editing process but sometime before the final book is released—to allow reviewers time to read it before the release date.

Banner: This is a small advertisement for your book, intended to be used for publicity on websites and blogs. Sizes vary widely.

Beat: A break or shift in the plot.

Beta Reader: Someone who will read your work critically before you submit it for publication to an agent or editor.

Blog Tour: A tour set up for a book where information about the book (and sometimes a unique post) appears on a series of blogs over a short period of time, usually to build buzz for the title.

Blurb (Book): A short (usually 2-4 paragraphs), high level recap of the book that conveys the set-up and introduces the characters but does not give away any spoilers. The blurb usually appears in marketing materials, on sales websites, and on the back cover of the printed version of the book.

Blurb (Series): A synopsis (usually 2-4 paragraphs) of the entire book series.

Brand: The net result of all your marketing, writing, and online presence – essentially, how readers feel about you.

Buy Links: The links to various retailers (like Amazon, Barnes & Noble, Kobo, etc.) who will carry and sell your book. Buy links are included in the blogger's tour stop of your book for easy access for the reader to make a purchase while reading about your book.

Character Arc: The emotional journey the character takes through the story.

Chasing the Market: The act of trying to write what you think the market wants right now.

Con(vention): An annual gathering of readers and writers, often in a specific genre or set of genres, that typically includes discussion panels, readings, signings, and book sales, as well as cosplay (dressing in costume)

Cover Reveal: An event to show off the cover of your new book, usually to help prime interest and garner pre-orders. We always suggest having your pre-order links up before doing a reveal so interested readers can order your book. Cover reveals can be on a single site (exclusive), or across a group of sites/blogs (non-exclusive). Some of the bigger venues require exclusivity.

Easter Egg: A hidden reference in the story that only dedicated readers will understand.

Elevator Pitch: A very short description that encapsulates what your book is about.

Evil Day Job (EDJ): What many writers call the job that pays the bills and is not writing.

Excerpt: (Exclusive/Non-Exclusive): A non-exclusive excerpt is a selection of your choosing from the book that offers the reader a taste of the book without giving away too much. Non-exclusive excerpts are distributed to every blogger who signs up for your tour. It's non-exclusive because it will appear on multiple blogs across the web. An exclusive excerpt is a selection from the book that is distributed by request specifically to one individual blogger to use to promote your book during the tour.

First Draft: The initial draft of a book, often a bit rough.

First Person: Stories told using I/me pronouns.

Fixit List: A list of known issues with your writing that you fix before sending off a final draft.

Flash Fiction: Stories of 100-1,000 words

General Data Protection Regulation (GDPR): The European internet privacy act that imposes stiff penalties for contacting someone by email without permission.

Happy Juice: That heady concoction made up of all the good things that have happened to us as writers.

Head Hopping: Jumping from one character's point of view to another in the same scene.

Holy Shit Moment (HSM): Also called the Eureka moment, when an important part of your story suddenly becomes clear to you.

Hybrid Author: Someone who both indie publishes and has books with a traditional publisher.

Imposter Syndrome: The feeling, common among authors, that we aren't "real" writers.

Info-dumping: Delivering too much information at one time in the form of narration.

Inner Critic: The little voice in your head that tells you your writing sucks.

Meme: A meme is like a banner, but generally has more text—a sentence-long excerpt from the book or a tagline or a good review. Memes are often square or squarish, and are basically a teaser or bite-sized morsel for your book, and usually include the book cover somewhere on the meme to help with book recognition.

Micro Fiction: Stories of less than 100 words.

Midlist Author: An author who will sell steadily but not spectacularly over a long period of time.

Muddy Middle: The heart of the story, where writers often lose their way.

Narrow: A publishing strategy of selling your books only on Amazon and Kindle Unlimited.

National Novel Writing Month (NaNoWriMo): An annual writing event in November in which participants are encouraged to complete a 50,000-word novel in 30 days.

Novelettes: Stories of 10,000-20,000 words.

Novellas: Stories of 15,000-50,000 words.

Novels: Stories of 50,000+ words.

Pantser: A writer who literally writes by the "seat of their pants," figuring out the plot as they go.

Plantser: A writer who does some initial planning, but otherwise wings it through the story. A hybrid of pantser+plotter.

Plot: The overall idea of the story, boiled down to the most basic level.

Plotter: A writer who figures out the whole plot of a story before they write it.

Point of View: The character whose head we are in as the story is being told.

Science Fiction and Fantasy Writers Association (SFWA): A professional non-profit association representing sci-fi and fantasy authors.

Second Draft: The part of the writing process where the author fills in details, smooths out the text and works out plot kinks.

Second Person: Stories told using you pronouns.

Sensitivity Reader: Similar to a Beta Reader, but with a focus on making sure you properly represent a particular type of person in your work.

Series: A series can either be a linked series (i.e., you need to read all the books in order because the story and characters flow from one to another) or a shared universe/loosely linked series, where all the books occur in the same "world," but often focus on different sets of characters. In a shared universe series, there may still be certain characters who appear in multiple books, but each story can be read as a stand-alone.

Series Bible: A document a writer uses to keep track of all the myriad details about their fictional world.

Shared Universe: See *Series*.

Short Stories: Stories of 1000-10,000 words.

Slush Pile: The file of unread, unsolicited manuscripts that all big publishers have.

Standalone Book: A book that is complete in and of itself. It can also be part of a series, if it can be read without reading the other books.

Sub-Genre: A categorization under the primary genre that indicates a particular type of story - ie: slasher fiction under horror, or steampunk under fantasy or sci-fi.

Technobabble: When a writer throws in a bunch of high-tech words to make their story sound all science-y.

Third Draft: The part where the writer incorporates beta and sensitivity reader feedback and preps the final manuscript for submission or publication.

Third Person: Stories told using he/she/it pronouns

Tour Company: A tour company (or blog tour company) is an agency that does all the work of setting up a book tour for you. Many blog tour companies can also help your book get reviews, and do cover reveals too.

Traditional Publisher: A press (large or small) that publishes work by a number of authors, as opposed to an indie or self published author.

Unique Post: A unique post is a written work that is supplied to one blogger for their exclusive use during the tour – this is often preferred for SEO (Search Engine Optimization) purposes. In other words, Google likes it when a blog post is unique. Examples of unique posts are an exclusive excerpt from your book, an interview with the author or a character(s), a guest post that you write with background or history of writing your book, creating characters, the setting, the tone of the book, your writing process, etc.

Vanity Press: A "publisher" who generally only provides printing and basic editorial/marketing services, and is paid by the author for these.

Wide: A publishing strategy of selling your books through multiple vendors, not just Amazon.

Wolf Under the Table: Shorthand for adding an unexpected twist in the story.

World-Building: Creating the feeling of your story world using descriptive detail.

Work in Progress (WIP): The current story you are working on.

Writer's Wait: My version of writer's block, usually your brain telling you something is wrong with the story.

ABOUT THE AUTHOR

Scott lives with his husband of more than three decades in a leafy Sacramento, California suburb, in a little yellow house with a brick fireplace and a couple pink flamingoes out front. He has always inhabited the space between the *here and now* and the *what could be*. Indoctrinated into fantasy and sci fi by his mother at the tender age of nine, he devoured her library. But as he grew up and read the golden age classics and more modern works as well, he began to wonder where all the people like him were.

After he came out at twenty three, he decided that it was time to create the kinds of stories he couldn't find at Waldenbooks. If there weren't many gay characters in his favorite genres, he would reimagine them himself, populating them with a diverse universe of characters. He would subvert them and remake them to his own ends. And if he was lucky enough, someone else would want to read the things he wrote.

His friends say Scott's brain works a little differently – he sees relationships between things that others miss, and gets more done in a day than most folks manage in a week. Although he was born an introvert, he learned to reach outside himself and connect with others like him.

Scott writes stories that subvert expectations, that seek to transform traditional sci fi, fantasy, and contemporary worlds into something new and unexpected. He also runs both Queer Sci Fi and QueeRomance Ink with Mark, sites that bring people like them together to promote and celebrate fiction that reflects their own reality.

His writing, whether romance or genre fiction (or a little bit of both) brings a queer energy to his stories, infusing them with love, beauty and power and making them soar. He imagines a world that *could be*, and in the process, maybe changes the world *that is*, just a little.

He was recognized as one of the top new gay authors in the 2017 Rainbow Awards, and his debut novel "Skythane" received two awards and an honorable mention.

He runs Queer Sci Fi, QueeRomance Ink, and Other Worlds Ink with Mark, and is the committee chair for the Indie Authors Committee at the Science Fiction and Fantasy Writers of America (SFWA).

ALL OF SCOTT'S BOOKS

Liminal Sky: Ariadne Cycle

The Stark Divide | The Rising Tide | The Shoreless Sea

Liminal Sky: Redemption Cycle

Dropnauts

Liminal Sky: Oberon Cycle

Skythane | Lander | Ithani

Liminal Sky: Tharassas Cycle

Tales From Tharassas | The Dragon Eater | The Gauntlet Runner | The Hencha Queen | The Death Bringer

Other Sci Fi/Fantasy

The Autumn Lands | Cailleadhama | Homecoming | The Great North | The Last Run | Wonderland

Short Story Collections

Spells & Stardust Collection | Tangents & Tachyons | Androids & Aliens | Love & Limitations

Contemporary/Magical Realism

Between the Lines | I Only Want to Be With You | Flames | The River City Chronicles

Writing

Suck a Little Happy Juice

Audiobooks

Cailleadhama | The Autumn Lands | The River City Chronicles | Skythane | Lander

www.ingramcontent.com/pod-product-compliance
Lightning Source LLC
Chambersburg PA
CBHW070920120626
46546CB00001B/344